# i'll pay you ten camels

AND OTHER TALES OF A MOTHER-DAUGHTER JOURNEY

# i'll pay you ten camels

## AND OTHER TALES OF A MOTHER-DAUGHTER JOURNEY

CHERYL SMITH

# acknowledgments

*I imagine I am like many first time authors. I had no idea
how much work it was to write a book! The joy of writing gets
all mixed up with the "to-do's" of actually seeing your book in
its final version. Thank goodness for two very talented young
women who came to my rescue! Thank you, Kelly Spence,
my editor, and Erin Grimm, my graphic designer and overall
cheerleader. I now know the true meaning of "I couldn't have
done it without you." You both have a fabulous future ahead of
you!*

*Thank you as well to each of my children: Andy, Lauren,
Chuck, and Kelsey. Although the book is centered on an experience with just one of you, I'm sure you'll see in the pages those
glimpses of yourself that bubbled out. It's true that being a parent makes your heart grow. Each of you has given me priceless
gifts, and I thank God for each and every moment I have been
blessed to share with you.*

*Finally, thanks to my husband, Scott, without whom any of this
could be possible!*

# foreword

I HAVE BEEN A MOTHER MORE THAN HALF MY LIFE. Like many mothers, my experience has taught me a lot. Motherhood is more a verb than a noun; it involves a certain kind of energy that propels you in a new direction. I grew into motherhood; it's not a role that was simply bestowed upon me. Sure, it's a job, but not one for which you receive a direct assignment or, moreover, one for which you can look forward to a promotion.

Certainly the paths of motherhood contain pleasant oases of soulful tenderness. Who doesn't love rocking a baby, especially one who's peacefully asleep? Or observing a dreaming five-year-old snuggled in a favorite blanket, or admiring a budding ballerina lighting up the stage at her first recital? But the strength training for motherhood's mountain climbing is brutal, and there are many moments of fear and frustration that will whip you into shape. Just lose a three-year-old for one minute, or sit at a parent-teacher conference with less-than-satisfying results, and you'll begin to feel that maternal muscle definition building.

I pride myself on taking the title of "mother" seriously. So, of course I had goals. Admittedly, I have been guilty of being "that parent"—the one who lives vicariously through her children. But doesn't every parent?

After all, wasn't *my* heart also beating out of my chest at a track meet? Weren't *my* nerves just as frazzled at a piano recital? Wasn't *my* sweat also dripping onto the court at a tennis match? Tell me you can't relate, parents; I dare you.

But despite any of my own agendas, I tried to support and celebrate each child's unique gifts above all else. Ball games, dance performances, piano recitals, musicals, plays, and teacher conferences filled my days (not to mention all the cooking in between). Those days blurred into weeks, and weeks into years. All that time previously spent in a personal bubble raising my own consciousness was no more.

I think any mother would agree that parenthood is tiring. Physically, mentally, emotionally, and spiritually tiring. But what do you do when you're tired? You rest. Sometimes you literally rest, babe in arms, lying on the couch watching a football game on a Sunday afternoon. Dishes pile up. Lists beg to be checked, phone calls returned, showers taken. (Was that two days ago or three?) Other times, you pass out, arriving home from some distant town in the early morning hours having witnessed a cold, rainy, and very unsuccessful soccer tournament. Either way, the memories are precious, and they build upon one another like stairsteps that rise toward parental perfection. You never arrive, but the rest sure helps you to take the next step.

It's in those moments of repose between all the practices and performances and other obligations where the memories really grow in fertile ground. Bedtime prayers and stories, tickles, vacations, surprises, celebrations, and simply time spent together combine to write their own story of how to raise a child. As my children have grown, I've realized that raising them has also "raised" me. Being a parent has chiseled away at my inner ego at least as much as it has shaped my children. And I'm so much better off for it. Like sharp cliffs gradually weathered by the elements without appearing to change from day to day, I have remained the same yet different. The waves of parenthood have softened the edges; I am more malleable and accepting. And now that my children have grown, I am finding joy in reinventing my relationships with them as adults—now that I have the time.

A special opportunity for re-invention came during the course of a unique journey with my second child and first daughter, Lauren. A shared trip to Cyprus and Turkey provided the perfect environment of mystery and enchantment in which to cultivate a new type of mother-daughter relationship. A new story was to be written. As fellow travelers, Lauren and I were poised to discover one another in a new way, although we might not have realized that at the outset.

Friendship, beyond what I believe to be typical of most mothers and daughters, was born on this trip. Expectation, acceptance, humor, faith, and growth were the stepping stones upon which we walked to find this treasure. Our journey will forever live as my perfect metaphor for the discovery of this very special relationship—the friendship of a mother and daughter.

CHAPTER ONE

# like mother, like daughter

—

AS A YOUNG MOTHER, I treasured the distraction that writing provided. I wrote a lot, mostly in the morning before the rest of the household came to life. Some of my words were prayers, some were more like diary entries, and some read like to-do lists. I wrote in journals which today stand in dusty mountains at the top of my closet. I suppose some of them might embarrass me at the very least and provoke misunderstanding at the worst, if they were read without the benefit of any explanation. Yet, my journals record precious reflections about my children that, for me, conjure up past memories which transcend time and space. I guess that's why I've never gotten rid of one of them.

When my second child, Lauren, was born, I spent a lot of time writing, releasing thoughts and feelings that bubbled to the surface. My husband, Scott, traveled a lot in those days, and I often didn't have much energy left at the end of the day to do anything that required physical effort. You see, Lauren never slept. You'll hear more about it, I promise. Indeed, the ebb and flow of the mother-daughter relationship is tumultuous, riding waves of sheer adoration to heated exasperation to downright outrage, and then back again to steadfast and unremitting love. (Not to mention the rolling of the eyes.) But it always comes back to love.

I didn't know any of this when I started. All I knew was that I had borne an angel, and our relationship was only a promise in the early days. As time went on, my writing reflected how a promise gets kept. It isn't always easy, but one thing is for sure: No one stays the same as when they started. In the end, we both grew up.

As Lauren grew older, I began to sense things were changing between us. Was this to be a friendship? It started slowly, and when she left for college, we tested the newfound waters of empathy and caring that are consistent among friends. But I could never drop my role as emotional caretaker, nor could I deny my unconditional love for her.

There's an old Chinese proverb that states, "One generation plants the trees; another gets the shade." While I was honored at the prospect of being Lauren's friend, I was always aware of being the one who had "planted the tree." Certainly she benefitted from this arrangement. I would be the one buying the new dress she couldn't afford. On the other hand, she'd have to learn to tolerate my constant words of wisdom. Friends just don't interact in these ways—but mothers and daughters do.

It was during this process of discovering what it meant to have a daughter on the brink of adulthood that Lauren celebrated her 22nd birthday without me in Cyprus. We had never spent her birthday apart, and I missed her. It seemed like the perfect opportunity to share the journal I had begun on her three-month birthday. She later told me she had taken the pages to the beach so she could read them alone. That made me happy. It began:

> *Dear Lauren,*
>
> *First, let me begin this diary by telling you that I love you very, very much. A daughter is a special thing, and that's why I've decided to write this for you. I hope someday you'll enjoy it. I only wish I would have started sooner.*
>
> *—LETTERS TO LAUREN, MAY 9, 1987*

Lauren's plan for her final semester at the University of Michigan was to study abroad for those five months, eventually graduating with a degree in film. The decision-making process to take the trip had begun one year prior to her departure, more than likely inspired by a travel gene I contend she inherited from me.

I have always loved to travel. My own father traveled as a buyer for a department store when I was growing up, and I have him to thank for introducing me to the world outside my very ordinary Midwest neighborhood. Although my childhood travel experiences were domestic, I was nevertheless captivated by the glamor of plane travel. In those days, one was still obliged to honor the experience. We dressed up, were served good meals, and retained a sense of awe and wonder at the mystery of flight. To be transported across the country in five hours was still an utterly magnificent adventure.

The plane trip, though, was just the tasty appetizer to the main course. Exploring an unknown city and state activated my adrenaline level for days. Any time Dad took me on one of his trips, I did and saw things that left me wanting more and asking lots of questions. Skyscrapers in New York, sailboats on Puget Sound, and hippies in San Francisco are images burned into my mind that wouldn't have existed without those trips. My mind was opened to possibility by exploring other places.

And so it was that I approached studying travel materials with Lauren. I had always encouraged my children to try to travel while they were young and unmarried, before the realities of life provided a different agenda. Some parents understandably disagree with my encouragement, and Scott had been that parent on occasion. I admit, he and many other parents have a valid point. Travel costs money; 20-year-olds don't have money. But often their parents do, and there's danger in young people taking out loans. Who wants to start their adult life in debt? I can't deny the importance of fiscal responsibility, but I say, seize the day! You only live once! Travel is the greatest of all teachers! And other stuff like that.

To our surprise, the island of Cyprus was pretty financially reasonable for a full term away. Of course, as a loving and responsible parent, I needed to see that she was safe. At this point I knew nothing about Cyprus, naively believing it was closer to Europe than to the Middle East. A little research proved that I couldn't have been more wrong. Cyprus is an island south of Turkey. Turkey invaded the island in 1974 and currently occupies approximately a third of its northern part. It is dangerously close to the hotbed countries of Iraq, Syria, and Jordan. Its capital, Nicosia, is surrounded by ancient walls built during the Ottoman Empire and is split politically and geographically down the middle, one half belonging to the Democracy of Cyprus and the other half to the Republic of Turkey. It is the only such capital city in the world.

All of this made Scott and me nervous. We challenged Lauren to provide us with evidence that the country was safe. Luckily, this wasn't hard to procure. The Turks and the Cypriots have coexisted in relative peace since the time of the invasion, and it is a popular destination for tourists, especially from Britain. The study-abroad company had literally reams of information designed to soothe parental fears. I saw palm trees, salty seas, cliffs, caves, and mountains, and was enticed by the history. Of course I had a vested interest. We took the bite and said yes on one condition: A parental visit sometime during the term was required.

I volunteered. My wings were beginning to flap.

CHAPTER TWO

# taking off

—

I WAS ANXIOUSLY WAITING FOR MY FLIGHT. I checked and re-checked my boarding pass, reassuring myself that I was definitely in the right place at the right time. I had my phone, my handbag was close by, my carry-on was exactly the right size. Restlessness set in, and I began checking out the other people on my flight simply to occupy my brain.

It was the giggles that drew my attention. Four little black-haired boys, perhaps two to four years old, were playing a game of chase. I settled myself to enjoy the entertainment. Oblivious to their surroundings, the boys dodged hurried travelers as if they were nothing more than cracks in the sidewalk.

Their rambunctious antics felt like watching Saturday morning cartoons. Laughter and squeals were the soundtrack to a clearly serendipitous meeting. They approached one another with some shyness, not like brothers whose first instinct would be to push or tumble. Their grinning expressions suggested the bit of insecurity they undoubtedly felt. I saw it in subtle ways—a tilted chin and slight squint in one's eyes, another's finger moving toward his mouth as he contemplated his role in the game.

The boys were intent on connecting with one another in the way boys have since the beginning of time—play. The tallest boy presented a ball and teased the shyest boy by tossing it just beyond his reach. I raised my hands up under my chin, resting my elbows on my knees as I anticipated the next scene. What will this sweet little cherub do to prove himself? I resisted the impulse to retrieve the ball for him, even though it had rolled only a few feet from my reach. Out of the corner of my eye, I saw Future College Football Player take off, showing Youngest Boy the effect that a few months of extra age can do for one's running skills. I sat up and folded my arms in front of me, settling in for what was clearly proving to be a great show. Youngest Boy gave up his position of receiver with respect, jumping and shaking his hands to show the sheer joy of merely being included in the fun.

Meanwhile, I noticed their mothers, who were also unaffiliated, sitting on the edges of their seats. One young woman struggled with her infant in a stroller, desperately trying to both feed her baby and keep an eye on her toddler. I remembered that posture of readiness. You are at once grateful for the preoccupation of your young one yet prepared to step in if something goes awry.

Sensing a camaraderie with these other mothers and the experience of having been in their place before, I prepared myself for the inevitable. It happened. The boys had been flirting dangerously with the moving walkway only a few feet away. Finally, the temptation bubble burst, and Future College Football Player taunted the others by holding the ball over the walkway. My arms moved back, my hands gripped the edge of the seat, and a primal protective urge to rescue rose to the surface of my skin. I could feel my heart start to beat faster. Of course, it would be Youngest Boy, wanting to prove his bravery to the others, who would approach the entrance to the walkway. He appeared fully prepared to recover the ball when necessary. As he thrust out his chin and scampered toward the action, I held my breath. His little hand reached up toward the guardrail, his face breaking into a mischievous grin. "Go ahead, do it," his smile seemed to say.

As if on cue, all four mothers jumped out of their seats, sprinting to Youngest Boy's side. His own mother reached over the guardrail, grabbed his hand, and whisked him away from danger. He cried out, arms extended toward his newfound friends, but they merely looked at him with sympathy, their eyes locked in disbelief at her indelicate act of mercy. In the end, the other boys were grateful to be allowed to continue their game as their mothers returned to their seats, albeit watching them a little more closely in case they got any more smart ideas. I let out my breath and returned to studying my boarding pass with now sweaty palms.

Ah, "boys will be boys," as the saying goes, and that was a particularly captivating show. I shoved my boarding pass into my purse and sat back, staring nowhere in particular. Watching the boys' antics reminded me of my good fortune to have four children, two boys and two girls. I smiled and nestled into daydreams, recalling in particular one late October day in 1983.

My husband Scott and I talked about how many children we dreamt of bringing into our family. We were celebrating our first anniversary at a local zoo, enjoying warm air and sunshine. Walking got us to talking. Doesn't it always? The premarital marriage handbooks these days would likely deem us irresponsible, because I admit that we never really decided on the number of children we would like to have until after we got married. Hand in hand, filled with the naivety of the newly married, we strolled along the paths and talked of the future. We knew we wanted children, but Scott was slightly more uncertain than I. After badgering him past the polar bear exhibit and whining my way among the snow monkeys, he finally admitted that he wanted two, ideally one of each. This is so like him! The symmetry and balance of his nature steadies my impulsiveness to this day.

Looking back, it's easy to see that he believed his plan would be manageable, both financially and emotionally. Continuing our walk, we relaxed in the dream of our children and the fulfillment they would bring to our lives. Sitting on a bench in front of the giraffes, we laughed as the towering creature approached the tall fence that hemmed her in and reached her long neck out over the sidewalk. I posed for a picture and was delighted to see her calf running toward her. That was it for her, and she turned back toward her baby, Mother Nature's sense of responsibility taking over.

That instinct that called her so immediately to the calf mellowed my mood, and for a few moments I considered the magnitude of parenting, its challenges and its blessings. How would we be? Would taking on this responsibility change me, change him, change our marriage, change my way of seeing the world? I reassured myself that my own parents had five children, and I really was reaping the emotional benefits of having four adult siblings, not to mention lots of nieces and nephews. I knew my parents had no regrets despite any struggles. I wanted four children.

We continued to talk about parenthood that day, teasing one another about the risks and benefits along the way. Ending the day over dinner, we were content living in the ideal world of our future family. The one rift was over the size, but we arrived at my kind of compromise before the night was over: We would have four. Luckily, Scott has a sense of humor regarding my ability to compromise, or lack thereof, not to mention a heart large enough to love a *dozen* children as well as his strong-willed wife.

Scott comes from a classical nuclear family, including

mom, dad, older sister, and baby brother. Growing up in a small town, their family was part of a close community, which of course meant that everyone knew everyone's business. Part of their business included having to move around often, renting home after home without ever achieving the financial independence necessary to have a place of their own for very long.

Somehow this transient lifestyle contributed positively to Scott's character. He is the most adaptable and flexible person I know. He learned at a young age that life is unpredictable and that happiness is ultimately nestled in relationships. We met in college and have been best friends ever since. Our love affair blossomed out of this friendship, and our marriage seemed destined from the start to produce lovely fruit. Each of our children enlarged our hearts, and we learned to love and respect one another in our unique roles as parents.

My journey had begun, and I was alone in the airport terminal having left Scott at security, reassuring him that I would remain safe and promising to carry his love to Lauren. I fidgeted on the edge of my seat, glancing at the customer service attendant standing at the gate desk. She wasn't much older than Lauren. She was efficient and friendly, seemingly handling life at the moment quite well. She probably wasn't thinking of her mother, perhaps hadn't all day. It reminded me that while it was true I was traveling to visit my daughter, I was not technically going to visit a child. She was also handling life quite well. My previous recollections of princesses, forts, Barbie dolls, and trucks cracked the tension in my face into a small smile. My shared history with Lauren had only begun in those childhood moments. Today I was embarking on a journey that would create different kinds of memories. We were both adults. What would that mean?

Since I had never traveled abroad alone, my excitement was tempered with anxiety. I struggled to calm my nerves, taking a deep breath and closing my eyes. I paid close attention to the physical space that surrounded me. The buzz of the terminal hummed background music to my thoughts. For now, I had a row of seats all to myself which made me feel less claustrophobic, and for this I was grateful.

The uncertainty of traveling melted into a quiet melancholy filled with memories. As a mother of young children, I had managed to maintain a level of control, at least most of the time. I tended to take personal responsibility for their milestones and mistakes and had varying doses of pride and regret mixed into each experience. Winding my life all up into theirs supported this illusion of control, but it definitely took its toll. Trying to be five people all at once gets a little tricky, and eventually proves impossible. There were weeks where my role would quickly change from defender to jailer, from cheerleader to quarterback, and from teacher to student. I remember insanely screaming out, "I hate first grade!" while finishing up a project due the next day for my youngest. She was, of course, happily jumping outside on the trampoline while I glued yellow yarn to the head of a silhouette provided by her teacher. How I convinced myself this was necessary, I can't remember. What I do know is that it's hard for a parent to give up control when you think you know better. We don't always know better. Children have an intuitive sense in regard to weaving the strands of their own destiny. If we get out of their way, it's amazing what they can accomplish on their own. It took me awhile, but I finally realized the benefit of this truth and moved from the center of their lives to the periphery. My role was still in process, but it felt more like relief. It simply wasn't so bad, having your kids grow up and depend on you less. Not only did it allow each of them the freedom to become who they were meant to be, it left me to experience them as gifts. I didn't need to be in the center; in fact, I preferred it this way.

I had 10 more minutes before I boarded the plane. I retrieved my boarding pass from my bag and turned my attention back to the boys. I was relieved to see them safely returned to their respective places. Strollers, laps, and airport seats now confined their little bodies, and Cheerios, Goldfish crackers, and halved grapes began to sprinkle the floor beneath them as they munched away. I smiled again, feeling camaraderie with the mothers and fondness for their children, a supernatural wave of emotion. In this quiet moment I had been graced by their presence. Stretching my arms over my head, I relaxed and my thoughts began to drift toward my destination, Cyprus.

At Lauren's age, I had backpacked across Scandinavia with a girlfriend for five weeks. We traveled as free spirits, staying in hostels with no itinerary other than to visit all four countries. Looking back from a parent's perspective, I thought to congratulate my own parents for their sense of faith and trust that I would remain safe. Perhaps it was because times were so different; people seemed blissfully unaware of the dangers we now have come to expect in traveling. After all, this was a five-week journey during which I would not call home more than once. They couldn't have known that I would sleep in a park one night, get lost in Stockholm on another, take a walk by myself at 3 a.m. to catch the energy of the midnight sun in Finland, and meet plenty of boys along the way. I consoled myself that Lauren was having a far safer experience in Cyprus. After all, she at least had a place to stay. A voice in my head reminded me that I was doing the perennial "whistling in the dark" that parents do in order not to go crazy with worry, but I tried not to dwell on that thought.

Returning from Scandinavia, I began a position as a buyer for the same department store as my father. There, I had the opportunity to feed my hunger for travel and support myself at the same time. I never ventured anywhere too exotic in the five short years I stayed in this position, but my appetite for flight and exploring unknown places was sated. It developed my independence, and the diversion from the day-to-day tasks of office work helped me to love my job. Later, marriage, mortgage payments, and children naturally impacted how often and when I could travel. I gave up buying and tiptoed into the unknown territory of parenting. This was a journey that most certainly revealed all manner of new horizons. Becoming a parent is the greatest trip there is.

I never expected some of these new frontiers. Traversing day to day along the parenting pilgrimage sometimes feels like walking a dusty path of ordinariness, until one day you come upon a vista that stirs your soul. For me, that was my own spiritual life. I had always "believed," as they say. As a child, I sought out times of quiet where I could really talk to God. Even as a teenager and young adult, I paid attention to the divine presence, albeit with an unsystematic approach. So, while it had been there all along, my faith was more like a fallow field in the years spent settling into adult life. It had remained uncultivated while I was preoccupied with becoming an adult. But God knew my heart, and he knew how to plant. My children were each tiny seeds sown in fertile ground. I think most mothers can appreciate this metaphor even if they don't describe it as such. When you experience the wonder of birth, the remarkable physical development of your child, and the emerging personality of a human person, it can't be described as anything less than wondrously fruitful. Raising a child to become his or her best self simply doesn't happen in one good season of sun and rain. It involves weathering a lot of storms, pulling a bunch of weeds, and exercising a whole lot of faith and mercy.

I turned to God often in those years, eventually learning to trust and depend upon him daily, much like my children did upon me. God was my best friend. When people ask me to describe the relationship, I use the word "grace." I just love the way that word rolls off my tongue and the images it conjures in my mind. Grace was the stillness in which I rested; it was the comfort in the night as I rocked my sick baby. Grace rejoiced with me as I celebrated at my child's birthday party, grace enlivened me as I cheered at a sporting event, grace consoled me as I worried at a school conference or coped (often poorly) during a crisis.

I grew into my understanding that God is not a mythological wish grantor. Believe me, I tried to make God into that being. It just wasn't beyond me to pray for a winning outcome at a ball game. Eventually I understood that God is love in its truest form. I may not have always understood, but I knew his love was holding me up. I longed to pass this onto my children, so when the time came, I threw myself into their religious formation. I never felt I knew enough to answer the big questions. (Did Adam have a belly button?) I became convinced that my curiosity begged to be harnessed by understanding and knowledge at a higher level. I went back to school after sending the youngest off to first grade, eventually earning a graduate degree in theological studies, spending five long years studying the history and methods of Christianity. I was so engaged in my studies that my children marked the calendar on the day of my graduation as "Mom's Day of Change." Was I really that bad? Probably.

To celebrate my accomplishment, as well as our 25th wedding anniversary, Scott and I decided to visit Italy, the place that had fascinated me the most by far during the past five years of my coursework. It was our first trip abroad together since our honeymoon to Mexico.

Ah, Italy! Where saints stand with sinners, simple piety challenges extraordinary grandeur, and stories of steadfast faith confront heresy in a grand history of human belief. Italy became an earthly meeting ground with God, a corporeal altar of sacred presence. Being in this environment helped me to understand that grace was more than simply a descriptive word for my relationship with God; it could also be embodied by a tangible place. I could see, hear, taste, and touch it. After all, if I truly believed God had become one with the world, didn't that make the world a very sacred place? Didn't that hint at the subtle way God makes every place matter? Wasn't I feeling this in every inch of my being?

Yes, God abides in every place. Places like Cyprus. I stared down toward my lap. My boarding pass was beginning to smudge from the time I had spent handling it. Thank goodness the announcement to board was imminent.

CHAPTER THREE

# *taking flight*

—

*Dear Lauren,*

*You have started walking! You are so pleased with yourself—grinning from ear to ear whenever you take off. We are all enjoying your latest achievement. When you first started, you would just kind of push off a piece of furniture and practically run with no apparent destination in mind. Now, though, your steps are much more calculated, and you toddle with your hands up in the air to keep your balance.*

*—LETTERS TO LAUREN, FEBRUARY 1, 1988*

MY HEART JUMPED as I heard my name called out from the flight attendant's desk. What was wrong? One of the side effects of parenthood is that, given a choice between believing the best and fearing the worst, parents often choose the latter. I sprung up from my seat and approached the desk to learn my fate.

The young man smiled and reached out his hand, gesturing with the other toward my well-worn boarding pass. I looked down toward where he was pointing. "Oh, oh, sure. Here it is." One of my leftover insecurities from childhood is an overreaction to authority. I stumbled through my words. "I'm Mrs. Smith," I said, taking in a breath and lifting my chin, trying my best to look important.

"Good afternoon, ma'am," the young attendant greeted. While I appreciated his respectful tone, being addressed as "ma'am" always made me feel old. At least he was taking me seriously. He keyed a few strokes into his computer while I strained to look over the stand. I felt inordinately nervous during those few silent moments. Finally he looked up and pronounced, "We have a seat for you in business class." He handed me back my boarding pass. His practiced smile widened just a bit as our eyes met. It must have been something about the way my jaw dropped or my eyebrows rose to my forehead. He could tell I was excited.

"Really?" I was surprised. "Why me?"

"Your lucky day," he grinned graciously. Placing the ticket back in its holder, he wished me a good flight and fixed his gaze on the next person in line.

"Thank you so much!" Perhaps it was just another business transaction for him. As for me, you would have thought he was handing over his paycheck the way I received the newly modified boarding pass. I hurried back toward my seat to review the details, fearing my good fortune might be snatched away if I didn't behave like a well-seasoned traveler. And yet there it was after all: the travel gods announcing their presence in the simple decree, "Seat 3A, Business Class."

Yes, this was a good sign. I shuttled onto the plane as one of the first called and began settling in for the initial leg of my flight. I felt spoiled by my luck. Had Scott arranged this, I wondered? My heart warmed at the thought of it. No matter; all I knew was that this was a fantastic start to my trip. I showered grateful and giddy accolades upon the flight attendants, eventually saving myself from the embarrassment of oversharing by organizing my handbag and looking down. Traveling alone was stressful enough, and being comfortable on the flight seemed really significant, at least to me. I smirked with delight.

Prior to takeoff, my flight attendant (yes, apparently you get your very own flight attendant in business class) approached, seemingly seeking to ensure I was satisfied. Go figure.

"Would you like something to drink?" she smiled. I tried inconspicuously looking at my watch. Oh, what the heck? Did it really matter what time it was? Everything was about to change anyway.

"Why, sure," I said, trying to sound like I'd done this hundreds of times before. "I'd love a glass of wine." She smiled, returning in moments with my refreshment. Free glass of wine in hand, I began to relax and feel excited about reuniting with Lauren. It had been four months since we had seen one another, and we had never been apart that long. Maybe it was the wine, but my anticipation once more took a detour to the past. I stared out the window and allowed my thoughts to wander.

The day I learned I would have my first daughter is forever etched upon my heart. A late-term ultrasound had been scheduled to confirm the due date, and I had arrived alone at the hospital right on time for a lunch-hour appointment. This was my second ultrasound, a somewhat anti-climactic event compared to the first. I had insisted I could go alone, reassuring Scott that I would call him immediately after I was done.

I don't recall feeling any intuitive inklings that other mothers claim when it comes to knowing the gender of their child. I told people that I hoped for a girl since our oldest was a boy, and wouldn't it be nice to have a balanced family? It's not that I was particularly picky, and I said all the right things. "Dear God, as long as the baby is healthy, we will be grateful."

But if I was being honest, I longed for a girl. Oh, let's be frank: I *desperately* wanted a daughter. I smiled as the memory echoed in my consciousness.

As I lay on my back, the technician smoothed the warm, gooey lotion across my abdomen. I searched the images on the screen intently, looking for proof I was carrying a girl. The technician went about her work, pausing only long enough to click on an image and record measurements. In comparison, she seemed so calm. My own heart seemed like it was beating fast; the confirmation of life and another beating heart within me was exhilarating.

"Do you want to know the sex?" she asked. She had probably asked this question a thousand other times of a thousand other mothers, but for me, it was as if she were now my sister and we were sharing a moment of intimacy. I looked at her directly, willing myself to trust.

"Are you sure you know?" I hesitated, waiting for her response. Meeting my eyes, I am certain she sensed and shared the passion of my dreams for that moment.

"I'm sure." Her voice lingered on the last consonant, giving me one last opportunity to think, "Thy will be done," in my mind.

"Okay, then I guess I want to know." The curtain pulled.

"You've got a girl," she announced. A girl! Thankfully, my position didn't allow my body to react to the thrill in my heart, or I probably would have embarrassed myself. I felt a tingling run from my toes to my fingertips—an electric emotion that lit up the core of my being. I remember leaving the hospital (Had I been skipping? No, not possible.), the sole carrier of this earth-shattering revelation. Should I tell anyone? Or should I keep this delightful morsel of good news to myself and savor it like expensive chocolate? In the end, I could not contain myself and shared the news with Scott, but I must admit, for the next several weeks we delighted in our conspiracy not to tell anyone else, including our own parents.

The first moments and days of a new child's life are an empty carafe filled gradually with all the goodness life's fruit can offer. The sight of hair and skin and fingernails, the smell of newness, the sounds of need and pleasure all compete for the honor of being "the best thing" about a baby. Quickly, however, everything that is the same about most babies settles into normalcy. We became accustomed to the smells, the sounds, and the needs of our daughter. What emerged after that was her unique nature. Her eyes told stories. Her cries were a language of their own, and we knew if she was hungry or simply bored. She stayed awake more than most babies. Even as an infant, we began to know her as something infinitely more remarkable than "the baby." She was Lauren.

She arrived two weeks past her due date at 8 a.m., February 17, 1987. Her entrance into the world came precisely at the time of year when spring-like days begin to tease our winter-laden souls with promises of warmth and light. It's probably no coincidence, since she's personified this same promise as she has grown into an adult. Perhaps she would disagree, but I sense that Lauren hasn't really changed that much from her very first days and weeks. Her character as a baby and toddler infected my world with sweetness; she was enchanting, tolerant, soulful, loving, content, persistent, and seemed determined from the very start to leave the world a better place because of her presence. She has a sense of compassion that does not judge, pity, or rescue. She'd rather encourage and inspire others to reach into themselves for strength. She has a bit of a sharp edge, an impatience for lack of effort that has, at times, been misconstrued by others. And yet, I have never seen her completely give up on a person, no matter their mistake or character defect. As my daughter, she has taught me at least as much as I have sought to teach her.

*Dear Lauren,*

*I found this diary while trying to sort out all the baby books. I haven't written in a while. Where does the time go? You continue to open new worlds for me with your amazing attitude toward life. You are truly a special child, and at seven years old, you remain as delightful as you have always been.*

*—LETTERS TO LAUREN, MARCH 10, 1994*

The glass of wine went down fast. I sank into my large, comfortable seat, fascinated by the controls that responded to my desire for perfect relaxation. I wondered how many times in my life I had flown. Countless, it seemed. My thoughts drifted, more than likely in response to the warm and soothing effects of the now second glass of wine.

When I was 22, a mere three years before I married, thoughts of a family were still far from my mind. Little did I know that six years later, I would bear my first daughter. I thought about how Lauren must feel now at the cusp of "real life." Oh for goodness' sake, I reminded myself, she's probably not thinking about anything other than what the day will bring; that is certainly the way I felt at that age. The feeling of independence when you're living on your own for the first time is intoxicating, but doing it in a foreign country must be downright liberating. Lauren was having experiences and emotions in Cyprus that I could only imagine. Her excitement to share these things amazed and honored me. After all, I was 28 years older than she. I prayed I was up to the challenge.

These past few years, I had enjoyed basking in familiar rituals and routines and had set aside trying new things or taking any risks. It was comfortable compared to the busy years of raising children. Regardless, there was no doubt in my mind that Lauren and I were not exactly on the same plane, to coin a phrase, when it came to our lifestyles. And I was entering her territory. I was bound to try something new, and that was a good thing.

Or were we more alike than I realized? I wondered how my expectations had formed her. I asked myself how her love and dependence had affected me. She was one year old when Scott and I decided I would stay home to raise our children. I was offered a chance to accept a buyout for my position which was moving across the country to a new company headquarters. In the beginning, the transition had been difficult. I went from "doing it all" to wondering what I was doing. In most ways, being a full time mother was the most challenging job I would ever have. It's hard to describe the fulfillment one feels, though, at the end of a challenging day. The reward of, "I love you, mommy" provides the ultimate in job satisfaction. In most ways, it was the ultimate fulfillment.

We taught each other a lot in those early days and years. I learned patience, acceptance, and an enormous capacity to love a little girl. She learned the importance of a sense of humor in dealing with a tired mom, as well as an enormous capacity to love a mother. We have practiced this ebb and flow in our relationship ever since—even after she finally learned to sleep. Conversations have always been easy, and arguments have been few and far between. We were like separate branches growing from the same tree trunk. Our lives were entirely different, yet we were connected at the root.

"Hot towel?" I opened my eyes and edged up in my seat, awkwardly extending a numb arm toward my perky flight attendant. What? Already? I wondered how long I had slept. Looking out the window, I was surprised to see the sun beginning to rise. Checking my watch, it still read 1:30 a.m.—6:30 a.m. in Germany, the first stop along the way. It was evident from my watch as well as my fuzzy brain that I hadn't slept long enough.

"Thank you," I mumbled. My brain was thick, and I struggled with which limb to move first to avoid the most serious discomfort. Strange, when it takes a few moments to locate where your body hurts. The warmth of the towel felt good, and the realization that I was almost to Frankfurt was encouraging. I folded the blanket and moved my magic seat into a more upright position. I decided it was a good opportunity to review our trip itinerary. Lauren had at least allowed me the pleasure of planning some side adventures while I was visiting; of course, she would have had a hard time denying me. Mom and Dad's pocketbook still carries a lot of weight, and I was the one footing the bill.

My brief review revealed the basics. After a four-hour layover in Frankfurt, I would fly to the Cypriot city of Larnaca, where I would meet Lauren. Lauren had planned the first leg of our holiday, and we would be taxiing from the airport to the coastal resort area of Ayia Napa. After a few days on our own enjoying the sea air, we would journey back to the apartment she shared with three other young ladies from Pittsburgh. Their place was situated in Nicosia, the capital city of Cyprus. After some time spent there, our plans were to travel to Istanbul, Turkey, and finally Ephesus to finish our holiday .

My body tensed in excitement, and I felt the need to move. I took an opportunity to walk the aisles of the plane, expelling some nervous energy and warming up my aging muscles for what would surely be a trip to remember.

CHAPTER FOUR

# taking risks

—

A FTER MANEUVERING THROUGH the Frankfurt airport, spending more than enough time in airport gift shops, I was grateful for the relatively short flight to Larnaca. We landed around noon, the airport in full Saturday-morning-travel mode by the time I stepped out of the gate. Although the airport was small, it was bustling that day. I located the baggage claim which was separated from ticketing only by a half wall filled with plants and tropical flowers. Looking around, the sea of unfamiliar faces blurred, and the sudden moist heat felt heavy and close. I ventured toward the baggage circle and did my best to look confident. Locating my bag and hoisting it off the conveyor, I headed toward the exit that was only about 10 yards away. No sign of Lauren yet. Perhaps she was outside. I stopped for a moment to retrieve the cell phone I had purchased for international travel thinking I could call her. No service. Great. Where was she?

I wheeled my bags outside the small terminal, feeling invisible among the people in this foreign scene. Families reunited around me, greeting each other in Greek. The diesel smell from the small buses and taxis was pungent, and they crowded the small sidewalk. The palm trees gave little respite from the sun that threatened to scorch me in my overdressed state. I hadn't considered what I would do if Lauren wasn't there waiting for me. Luckily, I didn't have to wait for long.

I saw her first, emerging from a taxi. Taking a deep breath of relief, I gulped in her appearance. Nothing could have felt more refreshing. Tall and slender, long hair blowing in the breeze, she looked like a goddess. Throwing up my hands to get her attention, I could hardly contain my excitement. She looked beautiful. Her blue-green eyes sparkled, and her smile drew me in for a hug.

"Hey, Mom!" Shakespeare could not have penned more deep and sentimental words. It felt so good to hold her for those few seconds before she broke the spell and reminded me that the taxi was waiting for us on my dime. She grabbed my bags and deposited them in the trunk of the car. We were off.

Our drive was going to be an hour or so, and my sleepiness helped to set me in a trance as we rode along that afternoon. Lauren chattered with excitement, challenging me to talk about the trip, about the family, and moving on to discuss her plans for the next few days. I engaged for a while, but our excitement calmed, and we took some breaks in conversation to stare out the window. The landscape of the island was not what I expected. I had vacationed in the Caribbean islands, and this island was nothing like that. I had envisioned sand and hotels; colors of blue, green, and white; and … people. The road we traveled was flat along the edge of the island. The shoreline was rocky, and occasional cliffs pushed up through the hard earth. Everything on the other side of the road was beige and unpopulated, green hills popping up in the distance with clusters of small, unusual pine trees that looked like towers of upside-down umbrellas set one upon the other. Majestic mountains emerged in the far distance, imposing their masterful presence upon the scenery. It was beautiful.

I yawned and stretched out my arms in front of myself, intertwining my fingers. "Are we there yet?" It was a lame attempt at a parental joke.

"We'll be there in less than an hour, and I think you're going to love it." I wasn't sure if she was encouraging me or warning me.

"Do tell," I wondered aloud.

"Well, I was here with my roommates about a month ago," Lauren explained. "We stayed at a cheap efficiency on the beach and had an amazing time. I promised myself I would come back here with you and not stay in a cheap efficiency! It's called Ayia Napa, and it's on the southeastern coast of the country. It's famous for its white caves."

"Sounds cool. Is it mostly tourists?" I asked.

"Well, there are tons of hotels on the beach, but most

of them are kind of small and affordable, so that's where people like me and my friends hang out. A lot of Cypriot families come here on their holidays, though, and we'll probably see British people here too. It's pretty popular."

"I'm looking forward to it," I nodded.

"Plus, you'll really get into the legend of this place. Apparently, there was a hunter king in the first few centuries A.D. who discovered it. It's this huge white cave, and when he entered it he found an icon of Mary, the mother of Jesus. He felt so transformed by the experience that he converted the cave into a small church and then built another church on top of the caves to promote the presence of the icon. The church is still there and is a really popular tourist spot. People make pilgrimages there and everything."

"Oooh, churches. Love it," I winked.

"Right. There's supposedly some sort of spiritual mystery in these white caves that people claim affects you. Totally up your alley, Mom."

Ah, she knew me well. I wondered to myself how this "spiritual effect" would feel. Probably better not to set any expectations. I put my head against the seat and closed my eyes for some much needed rest.

Arriving at our hotel in Ayia Napa was like entering paradise. Positioned at the end of a long winding drive, our home away from home rose up from a sugar-sand beach and was surrounded by beautiful flowers in red, white, pink, and yellow. Giant herons, their feathers tinged with blush, wandered in and out through an open-air lobby. Waiters dressed in short sleeves and white slacks hurried with trays of colorful refreshments. This was going to be just fine.

"Great job, honey" I breathed. I peeked beyond the reception desk and caught a glimpse of the sea.

"This is the best sand on the whole island," Lauren explained, delighted that I was so impressed with her planning. We checked in and made our way to a spacious room with a view of the beach. Looking out from our balcony, I marveled at the beauty of this place. The foam that rose up from the water topped the rocks like whipped cream, and glistening sapphire waves burst open onto the sand.

"Are you tired?" Lauren asked. "You could rest if you want."

I thought about it. I really did. A nap wouldn't be so bad, but the sea … the sea was absolutely gorgeous, and the day was warm and sunny. "No," I insisted, "I think we should take advantage of the day." Donning our swimsuits and grabbing our towels, we headed toward the beach. I packed my floppy beach hat for good measure.

"Hope those sandals are good for climbing," Lauren mused as we walked along the lovely, level beach sand.

"What are you trying to say?" I could tell she was planning something. My "mother knows best" instinct simmered beneath the surface.

"I really want you to see the caves, and they're about a mile down the beach; plus we have to go down some pretty steep rocks," she explained.

"Well, I guess I have no choice, do I? These are the only sandals I packed!" With newfound energy, we walked the mile down the beach toward the white caves.

I've never been much of a risk taker, but I know I've been even less so since becoming a mother. More than likely, both motherhood and age have contributed to my cautious approach to challenge and adventure. My sense of responsibility really kicked in when I realized how much my children depended upon me. Also, it doesn't help that I am the oldest in a family of five children, the designated responsible one. And yet, I can recall times in my teens and early twenties when a "devil may care" attitude provided at least a little sense of freedom and oneness with the universe.

In my twenties, I paid two Mexican locals in Acapulco 20 dollars to pull me behind a Jeep on the beach. I really did! They attached a well-worn harness around my shoulders and waist, assuring me that once the rope was pulled taut by their rusty old Jeep, I would fly! Right.

Sure, there was a parachute, but these were the days before this kind of tourist attraction was available at every resort known to vacationers. These were just two guys who were probably the ones to invent this thrill ride 40 years ago. And we were not over water, but on the sand. I was scared, actually terrified, but also exhilarated by facing these fears. I had it in me.

Standing at the top of a small sandy hill, I remember gazing down first at the beach and then toward my feet. Coiled in front of me was a thick rope with apparent frays. I heard my chauffeurs cry, "Get going!" and remember how they instructed me to begin running as the rope uncoiled itself. My heart beating out of my chest, I grabbed my harness, doing as I was told. In one amazing moment, my body lifted into the air.

But this seemed different. I was much older, for one thing. I could use that as an excuse for sure. Oh sure, I've heard all the cheery puffs of consolation, like, "You're only as old as you feel," or, "Age is just a number." Did I believe it? Douglas MacArthur once wrote, "You are as young as your self-confidence, as old as your fear." Where did I fall on that spectrum today? Maybe it was just the word "cliff" that was playing with my nerves.

Finally, we arrived.

"Lauren, you can't be serious. Those cliffs go down hundreds of feet. What if I fall? Beside that," I complained, "There's no lifeguard! There's not even another human being down there!"

She laughed and walked with determination toward the edge. "You'll be fine, Mom. Seize the day!" (Did I say that? Did she hear me?) "No worries, I've done this once already, and I know how to get down. I'll help you if you need it. Come on! You're only going to be here once," she argued.

Guilt. Who would have ever thought she could turn the tables on me so fast? I decided in that moment that I would think no longer. Douglas MacArthur, this one's for you! Drumming up all the self-confidence I could muster, I decided that constant motion was the only thing getting me down that cliff, into that water, and swimming toward that cave. If I thought about the next step, my body would freeze. So I forgot my age and became the child, trusting in my daughter to lead the way.

Down we went, traversing one sharp-edged rock after another, descending toward water the deepest of blue. Swirling amidst the blue were streaks of bright green and white signaling depth, and the movement in the water hinted at life beneath. I was intrigued by the spectacle that grew ever more magnificent as we descended toward it. Moving down a cliff is much scarier than climbing up. The instinctual fear of falling really kicks in from this perspective. Supposedly, this fear is primal, but I would tell you the fear of falling on rocks is that much more terrifying.

I marveled at Lauren's agility. As for me, I didn't exactly leap down the rocks, but my controlled steps remained fairly stable, even more so when she was holding my hand. We were in this together, and she wasn't about to leave me behind or let me quit. My mustered self-confident spirit ended up saving the day. We arrived at a plateau without further incident and sat upon a flat rock, our towels providing a bit of respite against the harsh surface. The water was still six feet straight down and involved quite a jump.

"Now what?" I breathed long and hard. "We're really going to jump down there? How will we get back up?" I asked, still hoping a lifeguard would present himself. I needed another quote to get through this one.

"Stop worrying!" Lauren reassured. I think she finally understood the full effect of my paralyzing fear and decided to take another approach. Appealing to my long lost sense of adventure, she coaxed, "Mom, it's amazing, and you just need to do it! You've come this far," she reminded me with a glint of mischief in her eye.

This had to be the closest thing to a death wish I had ever experienced. But what could I have done? Not jumped? I took the plunge. With one last look up to where I had begun and another toward the cave, I jumped. Immediately, my body numbed from the merciless coldness of water, and I began to shriek. "Save me!" I laughed, flapping arms and legs to activate my internal body heat. In reality I was fine, warmed by my first round of accomplishment. "This is great!" I exclaimed.

Gracefully (of course), Lauren dove in beside me. We bobbed and laughed, sharing in my thrill of facing and overcoming my fear.

"It really, really is!" she agreed, and we spent several minutes treading water and acclimating ourselves to the cold. Then it was time to swim toward the cave.

"This way!" Lauren motioned, and I knew if we didn't start moving, we might just freeze in place, so I followed.

The plunge into the water was amazing; raw sensations took over my mind and body. The cold, the danger, the excitement, and the beauty made me feel alive and powerful. I was doing this! Truly focused on the utter goodness of doing something exhilarating and doing it with

Lauren. No multitasking here! Just living. I felt unbeatable. I felt young. After all, age is only a number.

We swam toward our destination, a cave stained white that beckoned us to enter. We maneuvered among the large rocks, careful to avoid scraping ourselves as we swam past. Small crabs scampered away, irritated at our intrusion. Lauren has an irrational fear of crabs. I saw them before she did, and decided not to let the moment pass without filling her in.

"Lauren! Those crabs are jumping off the rock!" I teased her. She responded with a resounding scream, significantly louder as it echoed off the cave.

"Don't tell me that!" she implored and suddenly seemed much younger than her 22 years. I guess this place has that effect on a person.

"Sorry," I apologized halfheartedly. Meanwhile, large seabirds and bats flew overhead, propelling us along. (I like bats about as well as Lauren likes crabs.)

The entrance to the cave wasn't exactly welcoming. The small opening was nothing more than an oversized crack that we had to maneuver our way through before we could actually swim  inside. Leading the way, Lauren pointed to places where the sharpness of the rocks threatened to skin our arms and legs. It took us several minutes, but we wiggled through to the interior of the small cave. The rocks and shells were iridescent and peculiar. Some of them appeared to be two colors at once. We hollered out, nervously listening to the echoes we created, not allowing ourselves to think for a moment that sea monsters may exist. (Okay, so that might have just been me. But this place was so strange and new, that a sea monster may not have really surprised me all that much.)

A small beam of sunshine shot through the opening of the cave, illuminating a small corner of the space, and we marveled at the gleaming whiteness of the stone. We swam toward it and turned our faces back toward where we had come from, the sun beseeching us to return. Or it could have been the coldness of the water pushing us out, I'm not sure. I was glad I hadn't set any great expectations for a spiritual experience. This was just plain freezing!

"I think that hunter king might have been seeing things," I joked.

"Right," Lauren replied. "I sure don't think he was swimming when he saw whatever he saw!"

We swam out of the cave and back toward the platform where we had left our towels. By this time, I was tired and struggling. We had swum a fair distance, and my lungs were having a hard time keeping up with my pounding heart. The six-foot jump we had made to get into the water was nagging at my brain. How was I going to get out of the water? I'm not sure we thought this through. As we arrived at the edge of the rock, I fought the urge to panic. Lauren climbed up first, showing off a masterful combination of balance and athleticism.

Layering our towels along the jagged rock, she encouraged me. "Put your hands on top, Mom, and try to get your foot into that crevice. Then just push yourself." Sure thing, Lauren. I briefly wondered which would be worse, freezing to death in the water, or bleeding to death on the rocks. I decided the latter would at least appear courageous.

Sheer determination mixed with fear of drowning kicked me into gear. I failed miserably on my first attempt, my foot slipping and hurling me backward into the water. That was it. There were no choices involved as to whether or not I would do this. I found a small ledge, pushed my foot firmly into it and grabbed onto Lauren's hand for dear life. All those years of paying for a personal trainer apparently had paid off, because I made it the second time. Or maybe it was just adrenaline; who knows?

"I did it!" I exclaimed, examining the scratches I had to prove it.

Lauren laughed, grabbing my hand and pointing up. "Look, we have an audience," she snickered. Sure enough, we had attracted a small gathering of interested folks who watched us from the top of the cliff. We waved good-naturedly, trying to imagine what they were thinking. Certainly it was worth at least a few minutes' entertainment. And it wasn't over yet. We still had to climb back up.

Lauren led the way, hysterical at my awkward attempts to climb and pausing only long enough to capture my antics on camera for posterity. Towel around my shoulders and ridiculous floppy sun hat threatening to fall off at any moment, I must have resembled an eccentric character from a Jack London short story. Oh well, that's the good part about turning 50; you really stop caring what people think. Well, maybe you stop caring a little bit.

As we reached the top of the cliff, one of our observers offered to take our picture. I felt unabashedly proud of my accomplishment and handed over my camera. We laid down a towel and sat shoulder to shoulder like two good friends. I kept my hat on for good measure, thinking it made me look more like I belonged on the beach. Taking back the camera, we thanked our photographer and began the trek back to our hotel.

I had taken a risk, and it hadn't been easy. I have to say, though, I learned something about risk-taking that first day on my grace-filled journey with Lauren. I had spent a lot of time protecting my children from risks. I did my job, buying bike helmets and fastening safety belts; I restricted movies and set curfews. But I taught them very little about the value of taking risks and how it can help you learn so much about yourself. Sometimes we need people in our lives to persuade us. Who would have thought Lauren could bring this out in me? But she did.

On this day, I learned by playing the part of the child and allowing myself to trust. In her easy way, Lauren encouraged me to jump, to step outside of the restrictions of my age, real or imagined, and learn something new about myself. Without that moment of presence in the sea with Lauren, I may never have reached this point.

CHAPTER FIVE

# *falling in love*

—

*Dear Lauren,*

*You met great grandpa and great grandma for the first time last week when they came into town to celebrate their 60th wedding anniversary. They just adore you! Can you imagine being married 60 years? It's hard for me to believe Daddy and I have been married for five. I love your daddy so much; I'm really growing to know what a wonderful man he is.*

*LETTERS TO LAUREN, AUGUST 18, 1987*

C AN WE AGREE THAT "LOVE" is an oft misunderstood word in the English language? "I love my new puppy!" and, "I love my new dress," aren't exactly esoteric in nature. But relationships can be. Parents love their children, who in turn love them back. A newlywed love is different than a 50-year-old love. Can you love your job? How often have I proclaimed that I love to eat? (It's true. I wake up in the morning from dreaming of food and plan my day around my next meal.) The Greek language is much more precise, distinguishing one meaning of love from another.

While Lauren got ready for dinner, I picked up the "Things to Do in Cyprus" brochure provided by the hotel and sat down to read. Written side by side were Greek and English explanations of local attractions and restaurants. What a nice touch! I had been exposed to a small amount of classical Greek during my graduate school days, so I studied the brochure to see if I could recognize any of the words. I couldn't, but I remember learning that the English word "love" had several connotations in Greek.

I searched for "love" on the English side of the brochure in order to compare it to its Greek form. There had to be something about loving food on these pages! Guess not. Nevertheless, my mind floated back to my studies, trying to remember Greek words that translated to "love."

Some of it started coming back to me. For instance, *agápe* is considered an unconditional, self-sacrificing, and active love, a general affection for another. It could also be described as the willingness to sacrifice for the good of the whole. It's not specifically a religious term, but it has often been used in that context to express communal love centered on divine relationship. Probably not what I was looking for relative to loving food.

*Éros* is the passionate and sensual love of desire. It's the same word for which the Greek god is named, a winged creature always armed with bow and arrow. The Romans called him Cupid. Not coincidentally, the ancient meaning of this type of love was spiritual as well as physical. Supposedly, he is the child of Aphrodite, the goddess of beauty and love, and Ares, the god of war. Poor guy—no wonder he appears so conflicted. Our English word "erotic" is derived from this Greek word. Possibly this was a little closer to my relationship with food, but not exactly (although I was getting very hungry).

*Philia*, the love found in camaraderie, signifies fondness and appreciation for another. Friendships, business relationships, and even loyalties toward family members could fall under this connotation. This was not the one I was looking for either. *Storge* is familiarity and fondness, also used to describe familial relationships. Maybe this is where the puppy and the dress would fit best, but I couldn't pull out of the Greek language how to express my love of food. Thankfully, I got to put off pondering this dilemma for another time, since Lauren was ready to go.

After spending the day relaxing on the beach, we were ready to go out on the town for the evening. Walking and chatting along the main road on Ayia Napa, we dodged scooters and taxis that seemed to pay little attention to traffic lights and lines on the road . Lauren extended her arm, holding me back as we began to cross the street.

"Careful, Mom," Lauren warned. I checked myself. It's hard to get used to looking the opposite direction for traffic before crossing the street. My heart stalled, thinking of the fate of other travelers who may have made this dreadful mistake.

"Okay, now!" she exclaimed, dragging me across the street. Upon arrival, I found myself in one piece.

Our carefree meandering eventually landed us at Palazzo Bianco Italian restaurant. Why we chose Italian food that first night remains a mystery, but the people, food, and charming hospitality of the island that evening were an unexpected delight. One would have thought we were family members. Our host greeted us at the door. His smile and gestures were casual and friendly. He was wearing a crisp white shirt, black slacks, and a black bow tie, a linen cloth hanging from his arm. Formality wove itself easily into the comfortable feel of the place. I think he knew we were tourists. Graciously escorting us to our table at the window, we waited only a few moments before not one, but three doting waiters began to serve us.

"Oh, you are English!" our first responder assessed as he opened our napkins and poured our wine.

"Actually, we are American," explained Lauren. She glanced at me as if to ask, "How could he not know this? Isn't it obvious?"

"Americans!" he exclaimed. "Why are you here?" he asked while throwing up his hands, clearly confused yet smiling at the same time. Apparently, visitors from the States are few and far between.

"I'm a student at the University of Nicosia," Lauren said. From that moment, we were treated with special warmth.

"You know Obama?" the second waiter asked, clearly impressed.

We chuckled at his naivety. "Well, no," I answered, "but we get to hear a lot about him!" Our new friends nodded and smiled; they were as tickled with our presence as we were with theirs. After our meal, waiter number three brought over two small glasses of Kahlua with his compliments. The others watched at a distance, interested in our reaction to their token of appreciation. We smiled and enjoyed, lingering over our drinks at the small checkered table and basking in the genial nature of the place.

Sitting at dinner on this island of grace with Lauren, I was enchanted when our discussion turned to thoughts about love. Earlier, I had tiptoed around the subject of her relationship with a young man attending the Air Force Academy in Colorado. She knew I had my doubts about their long-distance love affair, and her trip overseas had only made it that more long distance. It bothered me that they had not spent much time together, and I worried about her getting hurt. The wine and Kahlua had done their job well, warming hearts and tongues enough to really take on the topic.

Lauren was in love. She had met Matt in their freshman year through mutual friends at the University of Michigan, and their relationship developed across the many miles that separate Michigan from Colorado. Because they belonged to an inherently digital generation, they were pretty successful at maneuvering the unfortunate fact of distance and utilizing technology. Cell phones, texts, Facebook messages, and Skype sessions allowed them to virtually communicate and stay connected. As for me, an immigrant to this digital world, I most often just couldn't understand how they did it.

It really shouldn't have surprised me that Matt and Lauren had grown serious about one another. But it did. Their relationship seemed very private, as if it were growing in a petri dish. Imagine God combining an intelligent, creative, determined, engaging young woman with an intelligent, resourceful, quiet, and responsible young man outside the influence of the sometimes harsh and grating influence of family and friends. Their connection mirrors Lauren's own personality in that she is ferociously private. She always has been. In school, she was most content to be in the company of one or two very good friends as opposed to a crowd of one-dimensional fun seekers. I would describe her as a charming introvert, one of those rare individuals who can light up a crowd with her creative energy while at the same time she seeks out the one or two individuals with whom she feels she can truly connect and engage.

Still, as a mother, I have grappled with the reality of their serious commitment to one another. Lauren's private nature aside, I couldn't help but compare her experience to my own with her father 28 years ago. Unfair, for sure, but understandable if you're a mom. Lauren has often reminded me that the only ones who fully know and understand the relationship are the two who are involved. In other words, what I think I see is illusory.

"How's Matt?" I asked innocently, knowing full well I was looking for more than assurance of his well being.

"He's great. Really looking forward to graduation," she replied.

Sipping my Kahlua, I hedged. "Then what?"

"He's been assigned to a base in Florida. I'm so happy he's going somewhere warm!"

There it was, the old familiar lump in the throat. Lauren's insinuation that Matt's happiness affected her own happiness, implying a future together I wasn't yet ready to imagine. I felt myself brace to say the words that came next.

"How serious is it, honey? Do you two have plans to be married?" There, I said the "M" word.

"Well, no not yet. I mean, he's sure about me, and I know he's the one for me too. But I still have some things to do for myself," she explained.

Relief rushed over me. While I remained focused on Lauren's words, I initially felt caught up in this amazing contradiction present in her life, something foreign to me at her age: She was in love with a man, but the man wasn't her life. This explains it, I thought; this is the enigma I have been trying to understand. This is why they can continue to have a relationship outside of the comfort of shared space.

Our waiter appeared with our appetizer, tzatziki with pita bread. Italian restaurant or not, there were just some Cypriot traditions that couldn't be broken at table. We grazed as Lauren struggled to explain herself.

"It's sort of like the 13year-old girl who can't wait to drive, but understands that it just isn't the right time ... yet," Lauren suggested. "We've both invested a lot, not to mention what our families have done for us, and we know we have some things we need to do before we make that commitment." It was re-assuring to know that Scott and I had done something right, raising her to be a person who considered all the options and consequences. She was truly putting good thought into her relationship with Matt.

The sense of determination and self-respect that we had sought to inspire had taken root. She was no one else's person if not first her own. And yet, I thought back to my own lover 28 years ago. Technology or not, I know I would have been miserable without his physical presence. Love has the tendency to take on its own life, and though I was a college graduate with career goals, I know those goals could not have been accomplished by living apart from my beloved. I needed to face it. My reality was not Lauren's.

I wasn't ready to let her go. Listening to her words, I felt heartstrings snapping in my chest. Was this about my feelings towards Matt and Lauren's relationship, or was this more about me? Mothering a child is the journey of letting go. What begins in the peaceful, shared space of a body ripens to the fullness of expulsion in birth, continuing to grow and blossom into two very separate, unique creations. I had spent the greater part of my existence nurturing her into the person she had become today. Yet, this day I was beginning to understand that it was okay, what I didn't know about her. It was meant that Matt should touch her life more deeply than I. My trust in her could allow my maternal energy to be released from its need to protect. We could grow a new relationship.

We finished our meal, said goodbye to our new Greco-Italian friends, and headed back to our hotel. The night was warm and breezy. This time, the arm that Lauren had extended protectively while crossing the street nuzzled into the crook of my elbow, and we walked arm in arm amid the late-night tourists who had begun to crowd the streets.

"It's going to be okay, Mom. You can trust me," Lauren reassured, her gaze focused on her steps. I sensed her insecurity, her need to please me despite the confidence in her feelings for Matt. I turned my head to look at her and squeezed her hand. I nodded my head and gulped to keep back my emotion. She was, for one more moment, my little girl.

"I know it is, honey. I know it is."

I was amazed by how much better I felt. Letting go didn't mean our relationship would be less than what it was then. I felt strangely excited by all the things I had left to learn about my daughter.

"How about a nightcap?" I suggested. I wasn't ready for the night to end.

"Jeez, mom! I hate to tell you, but you're becoming a bad influence on me," Lauren teased. "Sure," she smiled. "Sounds like a great idea!"

CHAPTER SIX

# beauty

—

THE HUMAN CAPACITY TO APPRECIATE BEAUTY has always fascinated me. I remember a college professor suggesting in an art class that some people have a special faculty, almost like a sixth sense, that gives them an extraordinary ability to experience beauty. Makes sense to me. How else can you explain the wonder felt at the sight of a beautiful sunset? The awe that strikes you when you behold a masterful work of art? The swell that rises in your body as it reacts to the harmony in a song? A person could know the proportions of the human body down to a segment of an inch, could be able to describe every muscle and bone. One could even have a masterful memory of these things. And yet, there is still something that person would need in order to perceive the beauty of this body. What exactly is this thing that allows us to experience beauty? Whatever it is, sixth sense or not, I felt a surge in my comprehension on this beautiful island of Cyprus.

Lauren and I returned to the hotel that evening and entered the cocktail lounge, prepared to end our night with a taste of something sweet. We selected the last table available and sat down. Almost immediately after ordering our drinks we were delighted (at least I was) to see entertainers outfitted in traditional Cypriot clothing come in to join the small crowd that had gathered.

"Great," Lauren moaned, pulling the cocktail table in front of her and leaving me feeling a little vulnerable.

"What's wrong?" I asked, oblivious to the telescopic gaze of our master of ceremonies for the evening, the tallest and darkest of the Cypriot dancers.

"Don't you see?" Lauren explained, "This is going to be an audience participation thing. I can tell by the way he's scoping out the crowd."

"Sounds like fun to me," I said cheerfully, settling in to watch the show.

"Just wait," she said, smiling sarcastically and sinking into her chair.

The dancers were beautiful, dressed in heavy black, red, and gold brocade outfits a la *Zorba the Greek*. I was mesmerized by the untamed twirling and stomping of their feet. Arms lifted high, fingers snapping, the dancers entranced the crowd with the sight, sound, and emotion of their movements. My senses were delighted, color and rhythm transporting me to a dreamlike place where capricious images flitted about and thoughts trailed behind. Caught up in the moment (and more than likely embarrassing Lauren), I began to clap with the others to the beat. That was all it took for "Zorba" to turn his attention toward our table.

Watching as he approached, I realized what I had done. Shoot! Here I was, nothing between me and him. He had a direct line and had clearly singled me out as his audience-participation prey. Lauren was right. It was going to be embarrassing, perhaps even humiliating! I have never been known to be the life of the party. It's not that I wouldn't like to have a little fun once in awhile, but some trauma from my childhood must have left me with a severe case of reservation. My constant fear of self-exposure stifles any spontaneity I might feel that would encourage me to dance on top of tables. I smiled and looked toward Lauren, holding my drink in front of me like a shield.

"Zorba" continued toward me, while the other dancers shifted their attention to other unsuspecting victims in the small crowd. I realized I had no choice, and made the conscious decision to make eye contact.

But there was no contact. At least not with me. Our handsome Cypriot gentleman stopped in front of us and picked up our little cocktail table, moving it purposefully in front of me. Reaching his hand toward Lauren, he pulled her into the dance. She turned her head back toward me. Her eyes glared, and she mouthed, "I told you so!"

Ha! The joke was on her! Shaken out of my absent-minded

self-centeredness, I began to laugh. I pulled out my camera and snapped photo after photo of the enchanting spectacle. Lauren was the center of the charming display, her dark features and mysterious eyes reflecting the Cypriot dancers' native beauty.

—

*Dear Lauren,*

*Hurray! Yippee! Hip, hip, hurrah! I can't believe it—you slept all night! I can hardly explain how beautiful you looked this morning when I picked you up out of your crib. You smiled, and you were so warm and cuddly.*

*LETTERS TO LAUREN, AUGUST 31, 1987*

Every parent thinks their child is beautiful, and I am no different. From the moment she was born, I was taken with the purity of Lauren's beauty. It is soulful and speaks to you. She insists that she went through an ugly stage in her middle school years, but I won't hear a thing about it. Braces, glasses, unkempt haircuts—nothing could take away from what I perceived as a unique beauty in my daughter.

She's no princess, though. Her father fondly refers to her as his "boy daughter," not only for her love of sports and her tomboyish attitude, but also for the unapologetic way with which she presents herself. More comfortable in a sweatshirt than a skirt, along with a makeup-free face and air-dried hair, she is nonetheless successful at maintaining a sense of allure. This was my traveling buddy. I have to admit it was fun to shadow her.

Eventually, I got up to dance with the rest of the crowd. Lauren grabbed my hand as we joined in a circle, kicking our heels and lifting our hands with the others. The activity made our hearts pound and our cheeks flush. Spinning around the room, we clapped in time to the music and paused in place to watch as the dancers balanced glass after glass upon their heads while continuing to participate in the dance. We were amazed by their performance and equally delighted that the attention had fully transferred back to them. It was easy to join in the lightheartedness of the atmosphere, like a scene from an old Greek movie. I caught Lauren's eye, and she tilted her head, seeming to ask if I was ready to go. I was.

We left the lounge late, returning to our room and staying awake only long enough to put some tentative planning into the next day's activities. We were leaving Ayia Napa in the afternoon and returning to the apartment Lauren shared with three roommates in Nicosia. I opened the patio door to hear the waves, taking in the salty air one last time before we went to sleep. It had been a great day.

The next morning dawned sunny, but windy, and I decided to take advantage of Lauren's sound sleep by venturing out onto the beach one last time before we left. I quietly slipped on some blousy linen slacks and a sweatshirt. Unable to locate my sandals, I slowly opened the closet, causing the door to creak just enough to make Lauren's eyes flutter.

"Whatcha doin'?" she asked, barely awake.

"Sorry," I apologized. "I was going to let you sleep, and I thought I'd take a walk on the beach before we have to leave."

"Can I come?" she asked, unsure whether I wanted to be alone.

"Of course!" I reassured, happy for the company. She dressed in a flash, grabbed the sunscreen and a bottle of water, and we were off.

We walked out of the lobby and into the artistically landscaped gardens that led to the beach. Immediately we were blown back by a powerful gust of wind, causing our loose clothing to plaster itself against us.

"Whoa! This is ridiculous!" Lauren exclaimed. "We've never had wind like this here."

"Just our luck, I guess," I offered. "It sure does a number on the sea," I added, pointing toward the giant waves. "Let's go!"

We braced ourselves, walking headlong toward the beach. It was worth every bit of that effort. Perhaps the inclement weather had kept some in the comfort of their rooms that morning, although it's hard to imagine anyone could really believe these were poor conditions. Living in the upper Midwestern United States my entire life has certainly prepared me to appreciate even the slightest hint of tropical weather.

The outgoing tide had left the beach looking as white and sparkly as a fresh snow. The seafoam swirled, rising with the waves before it bubbled onto the shore, leaving a layer of small stones and tiny creatures that rolled frantically back toward their watery home. A cliff rose above the shore about a half mile down the beach, and we decided to make that our destination.

I was definitely beginning to let my "mother" guard down; Lauren and I talked like two friends. Pausing along the way to scrawl in the sand, we wrote love notes to Matt and Scott, taking pictures of our drawings before they disappeared with the waves back into the sea. I was touched by the transparency of this simple act, the idea that life's moments cannot really be captured and held hostage. In reality, memories evolve and often grow fonder with time. We continued on, greeting other walkers along the way and playfully dodging the surf. I paused to roll up my pant leg.

"It sure didn't look this far away when we started," I grumbled.

Lauren, waiting patiently for me to finish, looked up to see some beach walkers coming toward us. "Hey Mom, let's ask those people to take our picture," Lauren suggested.

Gratefully, we handed over our camera to a young couple who were more than happy to take a few photos. We posed, holding our hair back to stop the wind from covering our faces.

"Sisters?" The man was British and could barely contain himself at his clever attempt to endear himself to me.

"Oh no," I protested. "Actually, I'm her mother." The man

smiled and handed me back the camera. We thanked both of them and went on our way.

"Did you hear that, honey? He thought I was your sister!" I made my best attempt to swoon.

"Right, Mom," Lauren laughed.

"I know, I know," I said. "But you have to understand, I have to take what I can get!"

"Sometimes you say the craziest things," Lauren replied. "You're a beautiful woman, and I hope that when I'm your age, I am as beautiful as you are," she added.

I slowed my steps. "Really?" Clearly, I was looking for this conversation to develop to its full potential. I was 50 years old, and my image of female beauty was still stuck in decades prior.

"Mom, look at you. You are healthy, you take care of yourself, you are smart and creative, and people are very attracted to you." Lauren's eyes glistened; whether it was the wind or her emotion, I still can't be sure. She gave me a quick one-armed hug. "You're the most beautiful mom I know," she reassured me.

"Well, thank you," I stuttered, making a grand attempt at modesty. I don't take compliments very well.

We walked on toward our destination, and I allowed the sound of the wind in my ears to relieve me from any need to converse for a few moments. Beauty truly is an illusory thing. The idea that beauty is in the eye of the beholder carries weight. Such a strange concept, beauty. I reflected upon the beauty I had experienced during this past day. Dancing, music, nature, and human comeliness were all facets of beauty, yet none held its meaning completely. The one thing they had in common, though, was the ability to raise consciousness to a level beyond what is ordinary. Was I really beautiful? The answer now seemed beside the point. All my life I had chased the deceptive notion of beauty, and it was only now as a mature woman that I was beginning to understand. The only answer that matters is the one I had just heard. To be loved by another is to be beautiful in their eyes. To be loved is a beautiful thing.

We had arrived. Standing before the enormous rock jutting from the ocean, its ragged edges slicing the view of the horizon into triangular slabs of blue and green, I was mystified by its beauty. Brown, gray, and black chunks of obsidian hazed over with mossy green vegetation dripped silvery white fragments of foam back into the sea. I noticed there were more people out to play now. They walked gingerly up the rock, peppering its surface with their colorful suits of red and yellow and blue. We stood for several minutes, taking candid shots of children who played in the calm pool that had formed between the beach and the rock. Their mothers filled their cups and buckets with pretty stones and shells that they used to decorate their castles. Their laughter carried me to another time, another place, when I was a young mother building castles in the sand. Here in this place, I was blessed with the understanding of the most beautiful thing of all: The castle may return to the sea, but the grace of the place will remain. We will be to each other, mother and daughter, truly beautiful forever.

CHAPTER SEVEN

# Strangers and friends

—

*Dear Lauren,*

*You're 11 now and growing up too quickly. Your self-confidence shines! You are kind, compassionate, smart and athletic, a great writer, an animated speaker and performer—plus you're funny! I'm convinced you could do absolutely anything you set out to do! Everyone who knows you agrees.*

*—LETTERS TO LAUREN, APRIL 15, 1998*

W AITING FOR THE TAXI that would take us to Nicosia, Lauren and I entertained ourselves by watching people pass through the hotel lobby. It was now officially the weekend, and tourists quickly jumped from vehicles that pulled up to the door, quickening their steps in order to edge out the next customer in line at the registration desk. Giant ceiling fans breathed warm wafts, and the scent of flowers sweetened the air. Servers approached appreciative guests offering warm towels and cool drinks. I sat on a marble bench taking in my surroundings and daydreaming.

Peeping from behind a gigantic lily arrangement, Lauren pretended to spy.

"You look like a one-eyed mermaid!" I laughed, startled out of my gazeless stare. It was fun being included in her spontaneous games.

"And you look like you're about to fall asleep," she replied. "We don't want to miss our taxi in all this commotion."

"Perhaps we should wait outside," I agreed. Grabbing our bags, we moved to the sidewalk where we could absorb a few more precious breaths of sea air.

"I can't wait for you to meet my roommates!"

"Me too!" I replied, looking up. "There's our taxi."

We headed toward Nicosia, about an hour and a half drive, where Lauren lived with three young women from the University of Pittsburgh. Arriving in this capital city of Cyprus, I was intrigued by its liveliness. I had not expected a place so modern. While there were no skyscrapers, the buildings were made of shiny glass and steel, and the main streets were wide and clean. Young people walked hurriedly home from work. I had never seen so many gleaming Mercedes-Benz vehicles in one place before. Turning off the palm-lined main street, we traveled several more blocks to Lauren's apartment.

This seemed more like the picture in my mind. Her building was a small, two-story, yellowish apartment with black guard rails teetering off concrete patios. The patios appeared squished together, placed just far enough apart that I could recognize they were assigned to different units. The other buildings seemed locked into place by alleys that intertwined the streets. Cats were everywhere. They scurried under cars, dashed amid bicycles, and climbed among garbage dumpsters. Palm tree fronds dotted the tops of the buildings, and red and orange flowers grew in everything from sidewalk cracks to window boxes. Open kitchen windows released pungent odors of grilled meats and spices. The neighborhood was filled with the energy of everyday life and claimed a distinctive Mediterranean flair.

Emerging from our car, we paid the driver and pulled our suitcases to the front of the building. A rickety elevator slowly lumbered to the second floor. As the doors opened, music and laughter greeted us as we entered Lauren's home.

"Hellooooo!" Lauren beckoned as we stepped from the elevator. I encouraged her to lead the way, following along quickly so I didn't get left behind and stuck.

"Hey! Welcome home!" Kelley was cheerfulness personified. She looked like a princess from an Irish folktale with her alabaster white skin and long, curly red hair. Her blue eyes sparkled. Looking from Lauren to me, she offered, "We tried to keep the place clean for you!"

"Hmm, trying to figure out if you succeeded," Lauren teased as she set down her bag and reached for mine. They hugged, and Lauren turned.

"Mom, this is Kelley; Kelley, Mom!"

"It's nice to finally meet you in person!" I said as I hugged her. "Lauren has told me so many nice things." Kelley immediately endeared herself and left me feeling eager to know more about her.

As if on cue, Desi and "blonde-haired Kelly" entered the room, apparently returning from class judging by the books in their arms.

Lauren made the remaining introductions, and we settled in to catch up on the girls' days spent apart. Back and forth, their easy banter revealed their obvious fondness for one another. Desi, Kelley, and Kelly had been friends at the University of Pittsburgh before they decided to come to Cyprus. They had accepted Lauren into their circle immediately. The girls' laid-back camaraderie along with the warm breeze blowing through the open patio door relaxed me. Mainly listening, I was struck with how shared experiences in this fascinating country had connected these young women in a way no other life experience could. They even talked the same!

Distracted from their conversation, I looked out the patio window until my eyes settled on a gigantic Turkish flag that flew from the top of one of the high hills not too far away.

"What's with the Turkish flag hanging practically in your backyard?" I inquired.

Desi smirked, catching the eyes of her friends. "It's just one of their schemes to annoy the Cypriots," she explained with a tinge of sarcasm. "Wait until dark! There's an even bigger flag they created with colored lights!"

Desi is a nickname for Desiree, and her nature echoed the exotic suggestion her name implied. Dark and beautiful, she seemed the most serious of the four. She explained that her love of travel had inspired her choice to pursue a degree in hotel management, and she had been working toward that goal for several years during summers and breaks. Today she was anticipating a telephone interview with a hotel in the States for a job as a desk manager for a large chain in Pittsburgh. She was nervous, and her inability to sit still confirmed it.

"Really?" I asked with confusion. It seemed so childish for a country to intimidate another country with little more than Christmas lights.

"No kidding," Desi replied. "At least the Cypriots are mature enough to not let it bother them … too much."

The history of the Turks and the Cypriots is marked with animosity. The invasion of Cyprus by the Turks in 1974 is almost unanimously viewed by the rest of the world as a gross infringement of international law and the United Nations charter. In effect, the government of Turkey claimed that the invasion was a necessary strategic move to protect its own interests, and it seized a 35-percent northern section of Cyprus. Many, but not all, Cypriot citizens were forced to leave their homes, traveling to southern Cyprus for safety and leaving their homes and property behind. The ones who have stayed are mostly living in poverty. No wonder they're upset. This section of the country is claimed as the "Turkish Republic of Cyprus," not acknowledged as a real country by the United Nations, but tolerated by the United States because Turkey is considered an ally.

The girls continued to tell stories of traveling across the border, seemingly intent upon tormenting my intuitive parental fears as much as I was willing to take. Because the city of Nicosia is divided between Turkey and Cyprus, there are points where one can wander into Turkey without much notice. Officials don't even stamp passports. Rather, they stamp a piece of white paper that must be presented upon one's return into Cyprus. It's probably all really valid and official, or at least that's what I kept telling myself. In any case, it seemed very close to clandestine and dangerous activity for a young woman.

"Remember that Saturday we got up early to cross the border?" Desi quipped. "We felt like spies!" My eyes likely looked horrified, but wisely I held my tongue in order to find out more.

"Oh my God!" Kelly laughed. "I was so afraid there was some Turkish soldier hiding in the bushes ready to shoot on command!"

"Do I really need to know all this?" I whimpered. Between parent and child, I firmly believe some experiences are better left unknown.

Blonde-haired Kelly quipped, "You sound exactly like my mom! When I told her we traveled into Turkish territory, I thought she was going to jump on the next plane and take me home," she chuckled.

The quietest of them all, Kelly looked like a Barbie doll. On second thought, perhaps a cross between the Barbie and Midge dolls of my childhood. She had an all-American-girl look that sparkled. Her naturally streaked long blonde hair moved with her body like a slow-motion television commercial for shampoo, and she had delightful dimples that lit up her face when she smiled. She was petite in stature, but her delicate appearance reflected a healthy glow.

Leaning forward to show my enthusiasm for her insight, I agreed. "I'm sure your mom and I would get along famously."

"No worries, Mom" Lauren reassured. "There really aren't any soldiers lying in wait. People do it all the time! Besides, there isn't a lot to see there unless you travel to the other coast." She could tell I was feeling like a pathetic parent at this point, allowing my daughter to surreptitiously put herself in harm's way. We all know the stories of Turkish prisons.

I wasn't sure I felt like worrying about this anymore, so I chose to believe what she said was true. Thankfully, the conversation shifted.

The girls' apartment was incredibly compact, with one small communal space that counted as a living area and a kitchen, plus two impossibly tiny bedrooms. The floors were laid with large white tiles with failing grout lines, and the furniture was hard orange vinyl. Not exactly the Ritz. The bathroom was equipped with a tank that held a ration of water for the week. Blonde Kelly explained that we couldn't run the water unless absolutely necessary, for it was a real possibility that they could run out before the week was finished. I was impressed with her nonchalant manner. Perhaps it was youth that allowed such flexibility; as for me, I felt my first twinge of homesickness. I can't even stand to camp. Admittedly, I have more than a few drops of blue blood coursing through my veins, and I have been accused of excessive daintiness and discriminating taste. Guiltily, I began looking forward to another hotel stay in a couple of days.

It was late afternoon, and it didn't appear I was going to be offered any refreshments. Turning toward the space that counted as a kitchen, my sense of order took a real hit. Dishes dominated the sink, clean pans towered perilously upon the stovetop, and assorted boxes of pasta framed the kitchen, threatening to spill their contents at any moment.

"What's with all the pasta?" I asked innocently.

Kelly laughed, and the others smiled. "It's the cheapest thing we can find to eat," she explained. "We're lucky if we can afford the tomatoes to put on top!" I had an epiphany.

"Is there a grocery store we can walk to for some snacks?" I asked.

All four girls looked at me like I was the food fairy.

Kelley, Kelly, and Lauren jumped at the opportunity for free food, offering to accompany me to the grocery store only a few blocks away. Desi needed to stay behind and wait for her phone call. We made our list, which included coffee, wine, and a replacement light bulb for one that had burned out several weeks ago. After all, what are visiting parents for? Along the way, I learned more about the girls and was amazed by their willingness to let me in on their lives. I was a giant care package sent from home, something familiar yet surprising, and delivered just in the nick of time. The girls accepted my presence as a gift, and I had an overwhelming desire to spoil them.

The grocery store we visited in Nicosia had two levels, and customers trekked between them via escalators. It wasn't too different from stores in the States, although I was a little unsettled by the unfamiliar cuts of meat that were displayed hanging from the butcher's counter. Veering toward the more appetizing array of fruits and vegetables, I began to feel hungry. The girls found me there, lightbulbs, canned tomatoes, and wine in hand. The blue blood surged in my system.

"Where's the best place to go for dinner around here?" I challenged the Kell(e)ys.

Lauren caught their expressions and held their eyes. The grins that began to grow on all three faces finally burst into one giant expression of pure joy. "*Meze*!" they declared at once, obviously reading the hint in Lauren's look that gave them permission to go for it.

"*Meze*?" I repeated, not familiar with the word and uncertain whether it was the name of a place or a food.

It turns out that *meze* is a traditional Turkish and Greek meal of many small courses that has a twofold purpose: to provide great hospitality and even greater food and drink. Think of it as an everyday Thanksgiving dinner. The food has wonderful variety and texture and is served in small portions, but the true reward comes from the sharing. Laughter and conversation are among the greatest portions of everything served up. It sounded perfect to me.

We finished our errands quickly and returned to the apartment to get ready for *meze*. I was excited. No plain pasta for me tonight.

Rimi Tavern and Restaurant is located in Old Nicosia, a pedestrian part of the city with brick sidewalks, patio cafés, and people casually strolling among the shops. We took a taxi to the old town and joined the small crowds gathered among the open-air booths. Here, the modern, clean lines of Nicosia were miles away. Life was much slower. Many of the proprietors called out, encouraging us to stop and look among their wares. Tiny Cypriot flags tied along a string banner waved delicately in the breeze along an alley. I was intrigued and pulled Lauren aside to a small textile booth located there. The girls continued on. Picking up a kitchen towel embroidered with "Cyprus," I showed it to Lauren.

"Isn't this sweet?" I remarked.

"Not too expensive, either," Lauren replied, examining the price tag and calculating the exchange rate in her head.

We continued handling some of the other things on display, unaware we had been noticed by the proprietor. An old man approached. He was bent at the waist and carried a rather disturbing countenance. He had a large nose, graying hair, and a huge mustache. As the owner of the shop, he had a vested interest in our reaction to the wares he was selling.

"Five euro." He appeared to be demanding money.

Not certain he was speaking to me, I turned around, but the only one there was Lauren. "I think he wants you to buy it, Mom," she explained, raising her eyebrows and lifting her shoulders to show she shared my confusion. She discreetly turned toward the entrance to the store.

Feeling a bit pressured, I turned from the man toward Lauren and began to walk away. Not willing to take "no" for an answer, he followed, eventually overtaking us and positioning himself between me and the sidewalk. Coming within inches of my face, he stared and shouted, "You are stupid!" Lauren and I were confused at first, having done nothing we thought would be considered offensive. We quickly began edging out of the booth and away from him. He followed and persisted.

"You are stupid, stupid, stupid!" he repeated, shaking his finger and hissing. We quickened our steps, only turning once to see if he followed before we caught up with the girls.

"Wow, I guess I learned my lesson!" I lamented once we had caught up.

"I'll say," said Lauren. "I wasn't sure if he was serious or not! What was he going to do next?" We shared the story with the girls, coming to agreement that shopping in Cyprus, at least in Old Nicosia, was not the same as in the States.

Luckily, the tavern owners were gracious and welcoming,

inviting us into their establishment and directing us to a lovely trundle table adorned with tulips and large carafes, begging to be filled with wine. We obliged and ordered two carafes to begin.

"Did he follow us?" I asked Lauren, cautiously looking over my shoulder.

"There he is!" she cried, and my heart jumped into my throat. I bumped my shoulder firmly into hers in irritation as she laughed at my expression. He was, of course, nowhere to be seen.

Our first course arrived, and we dug in. *Meze* is amazing! Tzatziki and hummus, eggplant, halloumi, cheese pie, chicken, sausage, beef, lamb kebabs, fruits and nuts, yogurts, and roasted vegetables—I had never seen such a display of food on one table. The waiters attentively kept the wine flowing, and our spirits rose to the occasion. Full stomachs or not, we couldn't get enough.

"How'd the interview go?" I asked Desi. We had rushed out of the apartment after our grocery shopping trip, food the only thing on our brains, and none of us had thought to ask.

Mischievously, Desi twirled her finger through her hair and grinned. "I got the job!" she spouted out.

"No way!" the girls shouted in unison. Kelley and blonde-haired Kelly were seated on either side of Desi and folded her into a group hug. We all raised our glasses for a congratulatory toast. She beamed, accepting her friends' accolades with grace and humility, reminding them of her luck and good fortune. They reminded her of her talent and intelligence. We raised another glass. I felt honored to be included in the celebration, tickled that the good news had frosted the cake of our sweet evening. Lauren had joined effortlessly in the heartfelt joy for Desi's accomplishment, helping me to understand what really great friends they had all become.

Finally, it was time to go home. We had stayed several hours, and the owners were now cleaning up around us. I tipped them generously, a gesture totally unexpected in Cyprus, and we ventured out into the warm night. Returning to the little apartment, the girls decided the night had just begun. I could hardly believe they were going out for the evening, but I guess that's the biggest difference between 50 and 20. Lauren begged off, and we decided we would stay in and watch one of her DVDs. Snuggled up together in her tiny twin bed, we held her computer on our laps and gave in to the desire for passive entertainment, just two girls watching a silly film about love, heartbreak, and reconciliation. It was the best movie I ever saw.

When strangers become friends, it feels like a reward for a life well-lived. I thought about this as I restlessly steeled myself to sleep that night. Lauren had left for Cyprus alone, her own best friend, and had gained three new friends since arriving just a few months ago. These girls were more than her roommates on a study abroad trip. They were a gift and would remain so for the rest of her life. I wondered about the man in the shop and how many friends he called dear. My guess is not so many.

I learned something new about Lauren that evening, and also something about myself. Friendship is grown in the soil of easy companionship and nurtured by compassion and kindness, watered by a healthy dose of humor. That Lauren had attracted good friends was not a surprise. That I had become one of them on this journey was, indeed, a grace-filled treasure.

CHAPTER EIGHT

# i had a feeling

—

*Dear Lauren,*

*You are becoming quite the traveler! Your second plane trip was yesterday. We are visiting Grandma and Grandpa in Minneapolis, and I was a little nervous about flying alone with you and Andy. But you both did great! I held you so close when we were taking off, and it felt like you were a part of me as the plane lifted into the air.*

*—LETTERS TO LAUREN, JUNE 6, 1987*

O F ALL THE PLACES I had thought I might travel in my lifetime, Turkey was not in the top 20. And yet here I was, on my way to Istanbul. The day had been uneventful up to this point. Lauren and I had spent most of our time re-packing our things for the four-day adventure to Turkey and had arrived at the airport for a complicated flight to Istanbul. Our travels would take us from Larnaca to Athens before we boarded another flight to Istanbul. It was entirely out of the way to go to Athens, but planes from Cyprus are not allowed to travel in Turkish airspace, so what was actually a very short distance turned out to be a very long plane trip. We could have swum to Istanbul faster, especially since we would have to go through customs not once, but twice along the way. Looking back, I should have taken it as an omen, since everything about this excursion would hold an element of the bizarre.

Our connection from Athens to Istanbul was delayed for several hours, and we struggled to maintain a sense of humor throughout our wait. It was nearly midnight. Using my handbag as a pillow and stretching out on the benches at the gate, I was uncharacteristically indifferent about my appearance.

"Okay, so now you're the official travel guide," Lauren reminded me.

"Right. And isn't this just an awesome start?" I mumbled through a yawn. Checking my watch, I wound my carry-on handle through my purse strap, attached it to my wrist, and closed my eyes.

It's true that I had planned this leg of the journey. While Lauren and I shared a love of travel, I had the benefit of a few more dollars in my pocket allowing me to literally "go the distance." This trip had percolated excitement in my soul since Lauren had decided to study in Cyprus almost a year ago. As a junior at Michigan, she had poured over different programs. I was excited to go through the materials with her, dreaming of places as romantic as Italy or as exotic as South America. I wonder if there is a travel gene that can be passed on from mother to daughter?

It's been said that the world is like a book, and those who don't travel read only a page. I belong to that book club. These days, television and the Internet make us feel like the world is merely an extension of our living rooms. We can choose whether to engage or ignore via the click of a button. There are benefits, of course. Certainly we're pretty safe and secure in our living rooms. But can you really absorb the wonder of an experience when you're not really there? Doesn't everyone feel like throwing caution to the wind once in awhile and stepping outside their comfort zone … literally? There is beauty to be found beyond the comfort of our own homes as well—an Olympic skier on a mountain in Europe, an adventurer exploring the Australian Outback.... And while digital feeds can amaze us and even inspire our imaginations, they cannot offer the authentic experiences that real travel provides.

There is a feeling when you travel that is unsettling. There is a restless insecurity reminding you that while you are not the center of the universe, you are still connected to it all. You need human interaction in a bigger way that is not part of your everyday experience at home. I am guilty of the linguistic arrogance that plagues many Americans: I only speak English. It is humbling how many people in the world know several languages, usually one of them being English. I have found myself counting on it. Yet language is only one source of my insecurity as a traveler. Another of my disabilities is a lack of spatial awareness. Put me outside of my own neighborhood, turn me around once or twice, and I'll never find my way back. Maps confound me, and I normally manipulate them in convoluted ways that have nothing to do with the cardinal directions. Even then, I'm much better off if someone will just tell me to turn right or left.

And then there is the variety of the people one encounters while traveling. Culture can influence whether people are noisy or subdued, colorful or bland, friendly and outgoing or suspicious and discourteous. People are often the most interesting and unpredictable part of the travel experience.

Traveling in a foreign country can be like being a toddler experiencing the world for the first time. Color and peculiarity engage and entertain the senses, steering the mind to places it has not yet considered. People challenge your language limitations, frustrating you at the same time they delight you with their effort to understand. You learn slowly, and you get better as you go, looking forward to the next challenge because it was actually sort of fun. Travel is like that—leaving the familiar page of home to discover the rest of the story in the book. It is only unsettling because it is new. Once you begin to turn the pages, you just can't wait for the next chapter.

To study abroad in Cyprus was Lauren's decision, and much of that had been practical and based on cost. Scott and I challenged our children to be financially responsible, and one way we did this was by insisting that they pay for a good portion of their college experience. A study in Cyprus was, surprisingly, one of the best values in Lauren's research.

Knowing this was to be an entire semester of being apart, Scott and I had decided that at least one of us should go visit. Lucky me! Even before she left, Lauren and I had determined the dates I would be there and begun talking about the places we could see. Turkey conjured up colorful imagery that swung like a pendulum from the exotic to the ancient. A quick Google search gave enough evidence to convince us that Turkey would be an amazing addition to our adventure. We picked Istanbul, one of the largest cities on the planet, as our starting point.

Istanbul has a 3,000-year history that makes it one of the most interesting places on Earth. Originally called Byzantium, it was settled by Greek colonists under the rule of King Byzas. He had consulted an oracle of Delphi that told him to "settle across from the land of the blind ones." Surely, good old King Byzas had crystal clear vision, seeing how this location on the mouth of the Bosphorous Strait provided an incomparable position for trade and transport. Early in the second century, it became part of the Roman Empire, and in 306 A.D., Constantine the Great made it the capital of the Empire, renaming it Constantinople. In 1453, it was overtaken by the Ottomans, and Sultan Mehmet II renamed the city Istanbul. Today, it is the only city occupying two continents, Europe and Asia, and is inhabited by more than 13 million people. It is the largest city in Turkey, which became a republic in 1923. Cosmopolitan and secular in its personality, it flirts mysteriously with an aura of mysticism. The Islamic call to prayer rings throughout the day, and more than 3,000 mosques, many of which were converted from ancient Christian cathedrals, dot the skyline. Two beautiful bridges connect Europe and Asia across the Bosphorous Strait, a 20-mile channel between the Black Sea and the Sea of Marmara. Its shores are lined with palaces, ruins, gardens, and villages, making it one of the most beautiful and magical stretches of scenery in Turkey.

I was startled from my thoughts by the gate attendant's announcement that we could finally board the plane. Detaching myself from my carry-on luggage, I got in line to board with the other travelers for the relatively short trip to Istanbul. We landed at 1 a.m., found our luggage, and headed for the now familiar customs area. I was nervous.

"I sure hope our driver is here," I said to Lauren, feeling like the vulnerable American tourist that I was. As usual, Lauren was reassuring.

"I'm sure he'll be here. How are we supposed to know who he is?"

"Hopefully he'll have some sort of a sign," I answered.

Luckily, we got through customs without a hitch, although it was somewhat disconcerting to notice the armed military guards stationed in the aisles. We hurried past and scanned the area. Nothing. No one. Now even Lauren appeared anxious. The terminal was emptying quickly at this late hour, and I began to wonder how we would find transportation. Just then, a young man walked quickly through the door, and I could tell he was looking for someone. Sure enough, he had our names written on his documents, and we were on our way. Unfortunately, the driver didn't speak much English, so we missed an opportunity to ask questions along the way. After a short 20-minute ride, he deposited us at our hotel, the Gemir Palace.

"Thank you," our driver nodded, opening my door and gesturing me out toward the sidewalk. I longed to be able to ask him more questions. One, for instance, was, "Where is it?'

Lauren said it first. "Where is it?" she asked, peering through the window of the cab as I followed the direction of the driver's hand. Indeed, the Gemir Palace offered no splashy entrance. Hesitantly, we gazed through the darkness. My eyes were drawn toward the streetlamps that lit the storefronts along the sidewalk. There were no pedestrians. Looking up from the curb, I saw the entrance to our hotel situated within an opening not much wider than the door itself. Ornate black lanterns on either side illuminated the walk, and a large brass door handle indicated this was the place. As the driver opened Lauren's door, a hotel doorman emerged as if on cue.

"Can you imagine trying to find this on our own?" I asked incredulously, feeling a little like a character in an Agatha Christie novel. Thanking the driver, we followed the doorman into the hotel. It was like walking into the 19th century. The lobby was flanked on either side by two small sitting areas. Low lighting seeped from ornately decorated lamps, leather chairs embraced lavishly upholstered pillows, and mahogany paneling with wide crown molding was framed by heavy drapes dripping with long tassels. It all breathed an air of mystery. The space had a slow pulse as we moved tentatively toward the reception desk. I noticed a small secretary's desk with a computer on top, the only indication that we were on the same plane of existence as we had been before opening that door. We approached our host.

No doubt because of the late hour, the clerk spoke softly, reinforcing the illusion that we were lifting a page out of *The Murder on the Orient Express*. Lauren seemed to share my impressions and stayed close beside me. "Good evening, *madame*," he greeted. "We have your room ready for you. Here is your travel itinerary for tomorrow morning," he offered helpfully. "Your driver will pick you up at 8:30 a.m." He smiled thinly and directed us toward the bellboy who was holding the elevator.

Obediently we followed the bellboy and our luggage to the second floor. I tried not to think of anything other than my upcoming rest, for we were exhausted. Entering our room, I was surprised to see two twin beds. We Americans are so accustomed to our bigger everything! Beyond that, however, the space mirrored the enigmatic beauty we had encountered in the lobby. Gold and burgundy wallpaper formed a backdrop to handsome silk drapes and iron sconces that dramatically illuminated the art hanging on the walls. Our bellboy opened the large mahogany bureau to reveal a safe, television, and telephone, quickly closing the drawer as we nodded our understanding. It was as if he wanted to prevent the 21st century from making too great an intrusion upon our stay. I handed him his tip and he wished us a good evening, silently closing the door behind him.

"Wow," Lauren exclaimed. "This is awesome!"

"It's gorgeous," I agreed. "But is it odd that we haven't seen another human being besides the desk clerk and the bellboy since we got out of the car?"

"Mom, it's two o'clock in the morning! What do you really expect? "Lauren countered.

"I expect I'm really tired," I admitted. "This bed, small as it is, will feel wonderful tonight! I hope we can manage to hear our alarm at 7:30." I studied our itinerary for several moments. It indicated our guide was meeting us at 8:30 the next morning. "I feel like I could sleep the day away tomorrow," I said to myself. Lauren had already claimed the bathroom and was climbing into bed. I wasn't far behind her, and we both drifted quickly to sleep.

*Dear Lauren,*

*The most serious thing that's happened lately is that you were really sick. Daddy had left for Colorado and you had been fine all day. I had a hard time getting you to sleep that night, though.*

*Your breath was really short and you seemed so uncomfortable. Something told me there was something terribly wrong. But it was 11:00 at night! By the time I had made all the necessary arrangements and got you to the emergency room, your fever was 105 degrees. You were in the hospital for five days, and the doctor told me if I hadn't brought you in that night, you would not have survived the night with your blood infection. I still don't know why I reacted the way I did. Children get sick all the time ... what or who caused me to take you in?*

*–LETTERS TO LAUREN, DECEMBER 21, 1987*

It was the pounding that woke me. Startled, I opened my eyes and struggled to remember where I was. What was that? I quickly realized it wasn't a noise that had disturbed me, for the room was as quiet as a mausoleum. It was my own heart thumping within my chest. Something seemed wrong. I turned toward Lauren. She appeared to be sleeping, lying still, and yet something felt different. It was her breathing. Quick and shallow, her breath caused me to sit straight up in bed.

"Lauren?" I whispered. "Are you okay?"

"Fine, Mom," she managed. "I'm fine."

"What's wrong?" By this time, the mother's intuition that had been trickling through my brain cells was running through my veins like a river. I got up. Sitting next to her on the bed, I rubbed her arm. "You sure?" I asked.

"Something just scared me, Mom. Probably a bad dream," she reassured me.

I took a deep breath and walked to the bathroom. When I returned, she still hadn't moved. "What is it? Are you sure you don't want to tell me?" I turned on the light.

Her eyes traveled furtively toward the end of the bed. Rolling onto her back, she struggled somewhat to retain her composure. "So I guess you didn't see it, did you?" she asked, smiling a little.

"See what?" Of course, that's what anyone would have said, right?

"I don't know what it was," she admitted. "A light, a hazy light, and it moved. I couldn't tell where it was coming from. And it was cold. Aren't you cold?"

"What?" I laughed. Of course I laughed. "Oh boy, Lauren," I counseled. "This place is really getting to you!" In my mind, however, I couldn't help but return to the pounding that had awoken me. Was it my mother's intuition that had done that, or was it something else? One thing I did know was that Lauren was sincerely scared.

"Hmm, well maybe he's a friendly ghost," I offered jokingly.

"I know. Crazy, right?" At least now she was truly smiling.

"It was probably just a bad dream," I said. "You're really tired, and it's been kind of a weird night. I think your thoughts are getting the best of you," I said confidently. "Let's get some sleep. We have a big day tomorrow."

What is it about a mother's intuition that makes it such a powerful force? As I struggled to return to sleep, I reflected on the strength of the sensation that had awoken me. Despite the preposterousness of a ghostly encounter, I had to acknowledge an acute awareness of Lauren's fear. There was nothing else to awaken me, and to chalk it up to coincidence seemed wholly false. I turned on my side to face her. The breath that escaped her was now long and deep. I relaxed. Relieved that I was able to offer consolation, I noticed it was a little cold in the room. I pulled up the blanket and fell back to sleep.

CHAPTER NINE

# Turkish delight

—

The remainder of the night, short as it was, passed peacefully. After slugging down some thick Turkish coffee the next morning, we made our way to the lobby and waited for our guide to arrive. On this splendid spring day, the street outside our door was alive with the bustle of busy people traveling to work. There wasn't even a glimmer of the sense of isolation from the night before. Shopkeepers opened their doors to the sidewalk, and transient vendors hustled for space to sell their wares on the corners. Color speckled the view, splattered indiscriminately on clothing, flags, automobiles, and trinkets for sale. The sky was bright blue, and traditional Istanbul tulips brilliantly adorned the sidewalk gardens in vivid shades of orange, yellow, and red.

Our guide's name was Omar, and he greeted us right on time. Introducing us to a couple from Australia, Omar explained we would be traveling companions for the day. We were delighted at the prospect of new friends. Eddie and Francie were a middle-aged couple from Brisbane, Australia, and had been in Istanbul for several days. We shook hands and exchanged pleasantries as our minibus moved through morning traffic. They were both friendly, although Eddie tended to do most of the talking. He was tall and thin, and his skin appeared weathered by wind and sun. An expensive looking camera hung from one shoulder, and a well-worn satchel from the other. Like a model for a travel magazine, he liked to peer through his camera lens or lift his chin to gaze off at something more distant. Francie, on the other hand, was small with strong facial features that reminded me of the caricatures drawn by street artists in tourist towns. She was obviously the sidekick. Their accents entertained us as we chatted about what they had already seen and done. No doubt the day would be enjoyable.

We began with an exploration of old-town Istanbul. The Hippodrome is an ancient circus where horses and chariots were raced competitively, much like one would imagine from Roman history. While there, we gazed upon columns sent from Egypt by Constantine the Great and a beautiful snake-shaped monument originally used by oracles in ancient Greece to predict fortune or misfortune. While I listened intently to the guide, Lauren kept one ear on his voice, her eyes darting between the different pieces of architecture. Omar gave us some time to investigate and take pictures, so we meandered toward the oracle.

"Wondering whether it could work?" Lauren asked.

I paused to look closely at the serpentine monument before answering. "I guess I'm just fascinated by how easily people trust. I mean, did they really think all the answers would come by putting faith in a piece of plaster?"

"Maybe not really so different today," Lauren responded.

"True," I agreed. I began to think of all the ways 21st-century humans tried to determine their futures. Everything from crystals, horoscopes, and tarot cards, to fortune tellers who don't seem so different from the oracles of ancient times.

"Have you ever wanted to know your future?" I suggested.

"Definitely not. I'm much happier right here in the present moment."

She was right, but I can't say that Lauren doesn't sometimes get a little anxious about things. When she was little, the telltale sign was wringing her hands. It was how I knew she was feeling stressed about one thing or another. But as she's grown, she has seemed to eradicate the worry gene that so many of us are burdened with. Her approach and attitude toward life and its assorted predicaments is even-tempered and rational. I'd like to think she gets this disposition from me, but of course I would be wrong. I have to "choose" to be positive; Lauren was simply born that way.

Omar walked over when he saw us enjoying our conversation at the monument. "Would you like a picture?" he asked.

"Absolutely," I replied. Omar snapped away and then explained to us that since Constantine had been converted to

Christianity, he had chosen to use the monument decoratively as a fountain. Decoration or not, I was reminded of the human propensity toward the mystical and how it had been a part of our nature as a species since the very beginning.

"I do wonder how often they were right. The oracles, I mean," murmured Lauren.

"I'm not sure that's what really matters," I replied. "It seems to me that no matter who you are or what you believe, what you really need is for someone to listen to you."

Turning in the opposite direction, Omar pointed out the obelisk of Thutmose III, a 3,500-year-old pink granite monument that was in astonishingly good condition. It stood in the middle of the original race track. I was amazed by the fact that it was already about 1,500 years old when it was moved from Greece in 390 A.D. Eddie, our Australian friend, said what was on my mind.

"And they did it without any heavy machinery!" he quipped and then added "mmm," as if the sound of his hum was a verbal exclamation point.

"Unbelievable." Lauren agreed. "Imagine getting that on a boat!"

"Had to be a really big boat, mmm," Eddie mused.

Lauren caught my eye and grinned. Eddie's little quirk was going to be entertaining! I mischievously played along.

"How many men do you think it took to carry it? I asked Omar.

Omar knew his history and went on to explain not only

the number of men that it took, but also the process involved in making it all happen. Throughout, Eddie continued to nod and "mmm" at every pause in the conversation. Francie seemed oblivious to her husband's odd habit, standing steadily beside him with an interested look on her face. We, on the other hand, could hardly mask our amusement. I felt like a badly behaved schoolgirl with her best friend.

—

*Dear Lauren,*

*Can I tell you that sometimes I'm afraid you'll stop loving me this much? I hope we're always close and that you can always talk to me. I often wish we had more time together so that I could delight in you!*

*—LETTERS TO LAUREN, MARCH 10, 1994*

Raising children is serious business, and good parents strive to pass along values that will eventually result in a meaningful contribution to society. This includes setting a good example. So for instance, my vocabulary, which was dotted with colorful expletives in my college days, underwent a transformation as a young mother, incorporating words like "bottom" and "toot" and "shucks" while in the company of the kids. Worse yet, it eventually became part of my essence. Yes, I was the "gee, willikers" mom. But slowly and steadily, as your children become adults, you regress to your old ways.

Pretty soon, when no one is watching, "Damn it" pops out when you drop a glass, or something worse when you are cut off in traffic. For the record, I'm not saying this is a good thing. But it's normal. Eventually, your children catch on that you aren't the perfect parent, and everyone relaxes just a bit.

Laughing at Eddie with Lauren wasn't the most admirable aspect of my behavior that day. But the benefits far outweighed the cost. We weren't mean; our merriment was shared discreetly. And Eddie became ever more endearing as the day progressed.

From the Hippodrome, we walked a short distance to the Blue Mosque, a magnificent piece of architecture dating back to the early 1600s. It is noted for its six minarets that dominate the skyline (most mosques only have one or two). We removed our shoes and donned scarves over our heads. If the outside of the mosque was outstanding in its architecture, the inside was breathtaking in its decoration. More than twenty thousand Iznik stone tiles in bright colors of blue, turquoise, and red adorned the walls. Omar explained that each tile was worth a month's salary of a good Turkish doctor.

"Do they ever get cracks in them?" Eddie asked.

"No," Omar explained. "Each tile is original and in pristine condition."

"Mmm," Eddie replied. Francie slipped her arm through his and guided him toward the wall for a closer look.

Lauren and I approached the worship space, which was completely open and lit by a huge chandelier that cast dim light upon some men on their prayer rugs. I was moved by their posture and reverence despite the gawking of tourists. The men appeared to integrate their faith with everyday life. The Islamic call to prayer is known as the *salat* and rings out from all mosques as a reminder five times a day. Despite the fact that Turkey is no longer a theocracy, this faith-filled element of cultural practice remains stable. I wondered how our family's Roman Catholic traditions would eventually play out in our children's lives. Much like the Muslim and Jewish traditions, Roman Catholics tend to blend religious practices into their culture. This doesn't necessarily make us more religious, but it does say something about our values concerning religious practice. We don't eat meat on Fridays during Lent, we assign importance to material objects (palms, ashes, oil, and water among them), and we tend to celebrate in a very big way any time we observe a sacrament. (There are seven of them!) But while religious practices are surely important, these Muslim men reminded me to consider a more essential question: How does my religious life actually connect with my daily life? Making that connection was a life lesson I began to practice more "religiously" that day.

We paused as we exited the building for the proverbial picture-taking opportunity. Turning to see the mosque from this angle, I was overwhelmed by the immensity of the structure and the glittering tiles that decorated it, like jewels on a crown. Even as the photo was captured, I was grateful for the memory that would be forever ingrained in my consciousness.

Walking across the street to the Haggai-Sophia, a former Byzantine church-turned-mosque, we learned that this beautiful structure, famous for its enormous dome, now serves as a museum. Built by order of the Byzantine Emperor Justin in the sixth century, it stood as the principal cathedral for the patriarch of Constantinople until it was seized by the Ottoman Turks and transformed into a mosque in 1453. During that time, the Christian bells, altar, iconostasis, and sacrificial vessels were removed and replaced with Islamic features such as the mihrab, the minbar, and four minarets placed outside the mosque. Eventually, even the many priceless mosaics inside the church were plastered over. Only as a museum have some of these treasures begun to be restored, and today the structure stands as an amazing collision of two great faith traditions. We were awed while moving through the     cathedral-turned-mosque-turned-museum, gazing upon its artistic treasures.

"Oh, look at the kitty!" Lauren exclaimed as we made our way toward the exit. Indeed, a black cat sauntered toward our little group, rubbing against a giant marble column as he approached.

"Ah! I see you've met our resident cat," Omar remarked. "You're lucky, he doesn't come around for just anyone. He's sort of famous, you know," he continued.

"Why's that?" Francie asked.

"When your president Obama was here several months ago, he petted him and a photographer published a picture of it. It was on the world news services. Did you see it?" he inquired.

"Mmm, no, I don't think I did," Eddie replied.

"He's so cute!" Lauren spoke softly, bending over to pet the cat who was now weaving itself between her ankles. Lauren has an incredible soft spot in her heart for small creatures, and I wouldn't have been surprised if this was a highlight of her day.

Moving out from the darkness of the Haggai-Sophia and back onto the street, we rode our bus a short distance to Topkapi Palace, home to the sultans and harems of the Ottoman Empire for almost 400 years. As we entered through its marvelous front gates, Omar explained that at its height of existence as a royal residence, it had housed as many as 4,000 people, including the sultan, his family, his concubines, and his children, as well as both white and black slaves. That's a lot of folks in one palace. Four enormous courtyards, a harem, kitchens, the royal treasury, and other royal occupancies comprise this enormous palace. The treasures were indeed breathtaking, especially the jewels. The world's fifth largest diamond is on display along with the emerald dagger featured in the 1964 film *Topkapi*. Lauren and I moved slowly from one display case to the next, fantasizing and whispering about life as royalty.

From the treasury we moved on to a museum that held sacred artifacts, including a letter supposedly written by Mohammed, and even some of his beard! Other items claimed to be authentic included the staff of Moses, the sword of David, and the skull and arm bones of John the Baptist. I have to admit this caused more than a few head tilts as I contemplated how anyone could know this stuff was real. In the end, I reconciled my doubts by attributing these claims to the realm of mystery. I didn't want to ruin my newfound enthusiasm for faith!

Our morning had been full, and it was now almost 1:30 in the afternoon, well past lunchtime, in my opinion. Omar led us to a lovely little restaurant overlooking one of the courtyards of the palace. Eddie, Francie, Lauren, and I sat down, and Omar excused himself, allowing us to dine together and giving himself a well deserved break. Taking our menus from the waiter, I glanced over some familiar offerings, along with some that were very unfamiliar. Turkish cuisine has adapted since the time of the Ottoman regime, and its flavors range from Middle Eastern to Central Asian, with even a taste of Balkan influence. It was hard to choose.

"You've been here for a few days, Francie. What are you thinking about having?" I asked.

"Well, the shrimp quinoa sounds like it might be good," she replied.

"Mmm," Eddie agreed.

"Lauren, how about you?"

"I'm thinking soup. I wonder what Umach soup has in it?" she said hesitantly.

"Mmm, yes. I wonder too. Mmm," Eddie agreed.

Lauren looked down at her menu, seeming to concentrate intensely on its offerings. I could tell she was trying not to laugh, and I avoided her eyes.

"Quince stew?" I said aloud. "Isn't quince some sort of fruit?" I asked. To no one's surprise, Eddie added the appropriate punctuation, "mmm." Thankfully, he added, "I believe so. I think it's one of those fruits you can only eat when it's cooked. Mmm." Of course.

We each placed our order and enjoyed a delicious meal spiced by some delightful conversation. By the end of the meal, we were sharing comfortably about families, occupations, and our shared love of travel. When Omar arrived at our table to retrieve us, we were surprised at how fast the time had passed. Our next stop, he promised, was something no tourist should miss. We wouldn't have much time. We got up quickly and were on our way to the Grand Bazaar.

The Grand Bazaar is a feast of sights and sounds, colors and languages, trinkets and treasures, and is one of the oldest and largest covered bazaars in the world. There are 22 gates from which one can enter or exit this maze of more than 1,200 little shops. Omar reminded us that we would only get a taste of the Bazaar today and recommended that we come back for a longer visit at another time. He dropped us off at gate number 7 and told us to be back in an hour. There were hundreds of people milling about, and Middle Eastern music filled the air. The aroma of sweetness wafted out from the entrance, and Lauren and I gravitated toward its scent.

"Shopping!" she exclaimed excitedly. As our eyes adjusted to the dimmer lighting inside the Bazaar, we stopped immediately at the first shop.

The atmosphere I had presumed for shopping in the Grand Bazaar was something akin to wandering at a flea market. I imagined local vendors hawking cheap tourist gifts to be taken to unlucky family members who stayed at home. As such, I was unprepared for our first encounter.

—

*Dear Lauren,*

*You were a bride for Halloween this year, and I don't think you've ever been so mad at me! I didn't think it was so bad—an old cream-colored bridesmaid's dress from a wedding I was in and a decent veil from K-Mart. I even let you wear a little makeup! But it was so cold that night, and I made you wear your coat under your costume. You fought me all the way, but in the end it was "no coat, no trick-or-treat," and you gave in. I've never seen such a pudgy, pouty bride."*

*–LETTERS TO LAUREN, NOVEMBER, 1993*

"Oh look, Lauren. That would look nice on your finger!" I pointed to a large bauble in the window of the first store inside the grand arch of the Bazaar. Stepping outside the shop to greet us, the shopkeeper agreed with my opinion.

"Absolutely," Lauren replied. "It's really gorgeous."

"Right, and you could just tell Matt you bought your own Christmas present this year!" I encouraged good-naturedly.

The shopkeeper moved a little closer and took Lauren's

hand in a gesture of greeting. He smiled broadly, taking note of our Western appearance. "You like?" he asked.

"Sure," said Lauren. He motioned toward the store's entrance and welcomed us in for tea. I had read that this was a common courtesy shop owners extended to their guests, and to refuse tea was rude. But it was only our first stop! At this rate, we wouldn't get very far. We did the right thing. We walked inside and accepted some tea.

The shopkeeper carefully removed the ring from the glass case, and I took Lauren's bag around my shoulder so he could slip it on her finger. "Ooh, la, la!" I exclaimed as she held it out in front of her. "You really should have that," I cajoled. Looking at the shopkeeper who was now on his way back with a plate of biscuits, I asked, "How much for this ring?" This was going to be my first attempt at bartering, something I understood to be the norm in the Bazaar.

"You want in American dollars?" he asked.

"Yes, please." My response was reserved and nonchalant and conveyed none of the nervousness I felt in playing such a role. I couldn't believe how effortlessly the transaction was going so far. This was fun!

"Ten thousand dollars," he replied with one eyebrow lifted and an even cooler air of nonchalance. Some primal stress hormone was suddenly triggered in my brain causing my body to react with a giant hiccup!

"Oh," I struggled to restrain my next hiccup. "It really is beautiful." This wasn't so easy anymore. Lauren quickly removed the ring and handed it back to the shopkeeper. We set our refreshments down and began moving backward toward the door. The shopkeeper ruefully dropped his shoulders and turned back to the display case. Maybe he'd have better luck with the next Americans who wandered in.

"Thank you, *hiccup*, you have a beautiful store, *hiccup*. Maybe we'll be, *hiccup,* back." We turned and left, passing several more stores before we could even take the chance to look at one another.

"Ten thousand dollars!" Lauren exclaimed. "Who did he think we were?"

"Rich, I guess," I replied. It wasn't a moment later that we heard shouting coming from the shop across the walk. At first I paid no attention until I realized there were two young men gesturing at us. Standing before a colorful display of silk scarves, they waved and called out.

"Are you Adriana? Adriana Lima?" one of them asked hopefully.

Assuming they were talking to me (Who the heck is Adriana Lima anyway?), I smiled politely and shook my head. It wasn't until then that I realized they were looking right through me. In fact, I wasn't even in the picture at all. What was I thinking? Of course it was Lauren they were addressing! They probably took me for the baggage handler. After all, I was still carrying Lauren's purse.

Lauren laughed and kept walking. "You're not going to believe this, but I've gotten that question before," she explained.

"Really?" I asked. "I've never ever heard of...who was it?"

"Adriana Lima, a model who started with Victoria's Secret and is pretty famous these days," she said with some added patience.

"Oh," I teased, "so now I'm walking around with a supermodel?"

"Whatever you want to think, Mom," she answered.

"Frankly, it's not so bad being the mom of a model. I can live with it!"

Suddenly we heard the same voices coming up behind us, and I turned around to look.

"Please, lady, come see my scarves. Beautiful, beautiful!" he insisted. His friend stepped out of the makeshift shop, quickly walking our way with several yards of silk.

"Adriana, please touch," the first young man insisted. "Touch, touch," he persisted. "You must take with you! One for mother, too." Gee, thanks for noticing.

We continued walking, their shouts seeming to get louder the farther we moved away. I don't get Turkish sales techniques, so I have no idea if they were truly perturbed. But suddenly I was petrified. I looked at Lauren. She was giggling nervously, and I could tell she felt as vulnerable as I standing in the middle of the walk. We waved goodbye and quickly walked into a ceramics shop where we accepted some tea and took our time looking around. After a while, I looked at my watch, and we decided we had better start making our way back to the entrance. The Grand Bazaar is so massive that it is very easy to get lost. Promising ourselves that we would come back tomorrow, we dutifully returned to where our guide was waiting.

Returning to our hotel for a bit of rest, we entertained thoughts of how to spend the rest of the evening. I suggested a Turkish bath. Why not? Isn't that what the Turkish are famous for? Turkish bath, Turkish towel—it goes together. I had in mind a nice sauna and an even nicer massage. Lauren thought that sounded pretty good, and we read a little about it in our guide book. Our concierge recommended that we not return to the downtown area in the evening and said we would be better off at a local bathhouse within walking distance. He called to make a reservation for us, but it was too late. We would have to wait until tomorrow.

We decided to take a walk toward Taksim Square, which is at the head of a very long pedestrian street. Every kind of retail shop or restaurant one could imagine is located on this street. This is modern Turkey, where the beautiful people like to hang out. We joined in. It was a little cool and very crowded, so we walked arm in arm to stay warm. Well, maybe it was to stay warm, but I would like to think we were linked by a special closeness that day. Spending one-on-one time together and making memories that only the two of us would share made me fall in love with my daughter in a brand new way. No longer a baby, a child, or a teen, I could sense in her the flowering of a woman. A beautiful woman with a beautiful future. What more could a mother ask for?

CHAPTER TEN

# barely forgiven

—

THERE ARE MANY WAYS TO EXPERIENCE the sensation of being lost. You can lose your senses, lose track of time, lose your way, lose your sanity. But when you're a foreigner in a foreign land, the sensation of being lost extends beyond your physical whereabouts. There's nothing quite like feeling lost in someone else's culture. But I'm getting ahead of myself.

Saturday dawned, and it was another beautiful spring day in Istanbul. Pulling back the drapes, my first glance was filled with breathtaking color. The streets were lined with tulips, planted in narrow sidewalk gardens and public squares all over the city. Tulips have a significant place in Turkish culture and frequently appear in Turkish and Islamic arts. Maulana Jalaluddin Rumi, more commonly referred to simply as "Rumi," was a 13th century Persian Sunni Muslim poet and mystic who was born on the eastern shores of the Persian Empire in what is now Afghanistan and settled as a young adult in what is now Turkey. Considered the national poet of Turkey, Rumi frequently referenced tulips in his poetry, probably because he resided in Konya which today is where the flowers for the Istanbul Tulip Festival are planted. But tulips have long been recognized as a cultural symbol, likely peaking in the 18th century with the Ottoman elite class which coined the phrase "Tulip Era." Today, about 26.5 million tulips are planted in Istanbul, attracting tourists from all over Europe and Asia. Tulips of every size, shape, and color soften the hard urban edges of this modern city, brightening the streets as well as the mood of the passersby. Color has a way of doing that!

After sleeping without further ghostly visitations, we felt well rested and ready to take on our second day as tourists. Our driver met us at 8:30 a.m., and we headed for the Spice Bazaar. Smaller and quainter than the Grand Bazaar, the Spice Bazaar is more local by design, and the shops are more orderly, tidy, and well merchandised.

The smell hits you first. Spices are literally heaped on tables in myriad colors and textures. Aromas waft through the air, coaxing you to approach and gaze upon these brilliant earthly offerings. We shopped for nutmeg, cinnamon, and saffron, and happily sipped the apple tea offered by shop owners. Abundant flavors of Turkish delight candy begged for tasting, and yards upon yards of beautiful fabric and pottery were displayed artfully on shelves and tables set up in each shop.

I stopped to admire a small plate and was immediately approached by the shop owner. This culture is ancient, and it seems everything has a history that is thousands of years old. Ceramics are no different. The little old man proudly described Turkey as the "land of ceramics." Since the middle of the 20th century, ceramics have been mass produced to ensure quality and safety in handling. Beautiful and functional, the pieces I admired were of a style called Iznik pottery, the designs of which commonly feature natural objects, often tulips, and colors of bright red, turquoise, green, royal blue, navy, and white. I couldn't resist and readily handed over the asking price. I hadn't quite worked up the nerve to barter, and he was such a genuine and gracious host that I didn't mind paying a few extra dollars for my prize.

Also among the bounties of the market were exquisitely woven Turkish rugs boasting colors so exotic it caused us to stand back, as if looking at artwork in a museum. Our movements were leisurely and our steps slowly measured. There was no hurry on this morning.

———

*Dear Lauren,*

*One week from tomorrow you'll be four months old! It's hard to believe. The time has passed so quickly.*

LETTERS TO LAUREN, JUNE 10, 1987

So often we take days for granted, wishing them away while in the throes of young parenthood. We wish our child would roll over so that she would stay asleep. We wish she would learn to sit so she could entertain herself more easily, walk so we wouldn't have to carry, talk so we'd know what she wanted. Suddenly enough years have passed that you wish she would get her driver's license so you wouldn't have to drive so much, move out so you wouldn't have so much laundry. When is it that we reach the point where we wish time would stop?

I think that morning I felt this way. I would have done anything to freeze that moment, package it up and take it home with me for those times I felt lonely or unappreciative of my life. Color, laughter, hospitality, warmth, sweetness cut by spice, beauty in every object and person—it was all there in the Spice Bazaar that morning. For me, it was all reflected in Lauren. I took it in like air, and when I released it, my body relaxed in the promise the world offered me in that moment.

My browsing quickly escalated into acquiring. We walked from store to store, stuffing purchase after purchase into the oversized backpacks we had brought along for the occasion. I returned to the rug booth, eventually falling victim to the Turkish rug salesman, a really good one, who convinced me to purchase a small 3-by-5-foot rug for $750. Of course, that included shipping. That's okay; I would explain it to Scott sometime between now and the delivery scheduled in six weeks.

"Mom, when it arrives, you and I are going to just roll around on it for a while!" Lauren laughed.

"It's a deal!" I replied.

As we strolled closer to the center of the bazaar, we saw our guide who had been searching for us, apparently for some time. Sadly, our experience in the Spice Bazaar was officially over according to his timetable, although he promised he would drop us back off after the next leg of our tour when we declared we hadn't had enough time. Backpacks in tow, we quickened our pace toward the vehicle which would take us to the Bosphorus Strait, where we had scheduled a ferry tour.

The day was extraordinary, warm and sunny, a cerulean blue sky reflecting facets of light like diamonds on the choppy water. Brightly colored sailboats and rolling green hills split sky and water as we boarded our boat, a bright white ferry adorned by fluttering red and white Turkish flags. The banks of the strait flaunted 19th century palaces alongside more modern palace-sized homes. The views of ancient mosques were at times obscured by hundreds of sailboats that had come out to enjoy the breezy, warm day.

Istanbul is home to most of the mosques in Turkey, more than 3,000, and they are an architectural wonder to behold. Adorned with minarets and columns supporting several domes and half domes, they impose forcefully upon the skyline from almost every angle in the city. Most have great examples of Ottoman tile work, including those of the Iznik style that had been described to me that morning. What I hadn't known was that Iznik tiles also bear the name of the town from which they originated, so that the aesthetic of the town is preserved within the architecture of the entire country. As the mosques flickered in and out of sight beyond the sailboats, I considered how the separation created by even a small expanse of water can result in two completely different cultures—Europe on one side of the Bosphorus Strait and Asia on the other. The juxtaposition was amazing.

Sitting back on a bench under the open sky, the breeze rushing through our hair, we lifted our faces to the welcome warmth of the sun. For a few moments we remained silent, and I had a sense of oneness with the beautiful Turkish people. It was over too soon. The ferry lurched into the dock, forcing us to focus on the more mundane activity of gathering our belongings and making our way toward the exit. We deboarded the ferry, suddenly aware of the ache in our stomachs that reminded us it was lunchtime.

Just as he had promised, our guide was waiting for us and prepared to return to the Spice Bazaar where we had wanted to spend more time. When we asked if there was somewhere close by we could eat, he provided an alternative.

"If you want an authentic experience, you should visit the Bosphorus Bridge. There are two levels to the bridge, one for cars and trams, and the lower level for shops and outdoor cafes. Fish is our specialty, and you mustn't leave Istanbul without tasting a fish sandwich for lunch!"

"Will we be able to find our way back to the spice market?" I asked.

"Why, of course," our guide assured. "It is only a short walk, and you can see the spires from where you are. You will have no problem."

We agreed we were up for the experience and said goodbye to our guide at the base of the bridge, beginning our search for an enticing cafe. It occurred to me that this was our first venture into Istanbul without a chaperone to direct us. I quickly dismissed any hesitation, however, and put my faith in the advice of our guide. This would be no problem.

We found a place where plenty of locals were gathered and dutifully ordered the fish sandwiches. The look on Lauren's face after her first bite was one of horror. The fish was pungent, filled with tiny bones, and obviously not what she had had in mind. I admit it wasn't the best thing I had ever tasted, but I managed to finish most of mine, although Lauren had entirely lost her appetite.

Overcome by motherly concern that my child wasn't eating while trying to disregard the ashen appearance of her skin, I asked, "Would you like to try somewhere else?"

"No, I don't think I could," she replied. "What I really think I need is to get away from this smell and breathe some fresh air."

"Well, if you're sure you won't be too hungry..." I surmised, "We could make our way back to the Spice Bazaar." It bothered me that we had only had coffee and a small cake for breakfast and now she would be skipping lunch.

"You know what?" Lauren smiled back, "I think that's a *grand* idea!" She seemed refreshed and enthusiastic enough for me to forget my concerns.

We turned the corner beyond the bridge and looked down through the neighborhood. We could see the spires of the Spice Bazaar, so we headed in that direction. From there, I honestly don't know what happened. The streets of center Istanbul are incredibly hilly, and it is easy to lose sight of your destination. The day was growing warm.

Frustrated with ourselves and each other, we trudged with our now incredibly heavy backpacks up and down the streets, turning corner after corner with no success. There wasn't even anyone to ask for help.

"Mom, no, it can't be that way," Lauren insisted. "Your sense of direction stinks," she added with annoyance.

Only mildly offended, since she was embarrassingly accurate in her assessment of my skills, I found the self respect to retort, "If you're so much better, why are we still walking?" It had been an hour and a half since we had left the cafe. She was tired, and I was exhausted. Looking more than a little worse for wear, we considered giving up our search and taking a taxi back to the hotel. The next corner, though, provided some much needed rejuvenation to our spirits. We had arrived! The annoyance that had bubbled to the surface in the last few moments evaporated and we sped up with newfound energy.

Getting lost, especially when you know you're close to

your destination, is an aggravating and upsetting experience. My brain had battled with my body, which had battled frantically with my intuition. It's hard not to compare it to parenthood. I admit to often feeling lost, and not just in terms of direction. More often I was searching for understanding and friendship from my children, which was elusive in that I wasn't really called on to be their friend. What a relief to feel that congeniality with Lauren today. We were buddies. But there were times when she was growing up that I wouldn't have been the first "buddy" on her list. I had made some mistakes along the way that I still regret.

———

*Dear Lauren,*

*We need to find a new home for Tanner. It's heartbreaking to see you so sad about losing him, but I'm afraid I just can't cope with the extra responsibility any longer. I hope that someday you'll understand, and I hope you forgive me for this pain in your life.*

*−LETTERS TO LAUREN, MARCH 10, 1994*

Tanner had been the family puppy for two years. We had brought him home two months before we had our fourth child.. This was our first home, one that had seemed perfect 10 years ago but now threatened to burst at its seams with all six of us. I was seven months pregnant, focused on my burgeoning body and preparing the nest to receive one more chick. The timing on adopting a puppy had definitely been off, but like most parents, we lived for the days when our children bounced off the walls from pure delight. We truly thought we were doing the right thing. Surely, if we could handle three babies, we could train a puppy.

And they really had bounced off the walls with excitement! Tanner was an adorable Yellow Labrador Retriever with boundless energy and a doggone mind of his own. From the day we brought him home, though, I had trouble coping. Caring for an infant plus three children under the age of nine overwhelmed me, not to mention what the postpartum hormones were doing to my brain. Tanner was difficult, even on a good day. He had torn down wallpaper, unintentionally pulled our three-year-old's shoulder out of its socket , and generally gotten into mischief on a daily basis. I had missed the mark on this one and daily questioned my own sanity. Finally I came to the realization that if I was going to be the best mother I could be, it wasn't going to be with a puppy in the house. I made the very difficult decision to talk to Scott about finding a new home for Tanner. He agreed.

Tanner was Lauren's buddy. Of all the children in the family, her relationship with this puppy was special. She talked to him when she was sad;, she petted him when he seemed sad; and she fed, groomed, and played with him. For goodness' sake, she was seven! It's been said that seven is the "wonder year." It is the bridge from babyhood to childhood. Things change for children when they turn seven. They gain empathy and compassion, turning out from within themselves. I could sense her growing maturity in the way she treated me, her new baby sister, and of course her beloved pet.

It must have been so heartbreaking to lose her friend. It still saddens me to think I had to put myself and my needs before hers for the good of the family. How could I expect her to understand? I was lost in my fear. I didn't know if she would ever forgive me. I just didn't know. Luckily, we did find a good home for the dog, and we did the best job we could in transitioning him from one home to another. It broke my heart.

There is no magical segue that occurs in the transition from all-knowing parent to imperfect-parent-friend. Thankfully, the moments of forgiveness build like blocks, and the kept promises are like cement. Soon you have created a stable tower standing strong despite the mistakes that threaten to topple the relationship. So it was that we quickly forgot our petty annoyance with one another that day and approached the market, entering through the main gate. We felt a bit let down from the morning's visit. Nothing looked quite as appealing or colorful. The shopkeepers had clearly woken up and were at the ready to harass. It seemed more annoying than anything else.

"How many camels you want for her?" one particularly impudent shop owner cried out. He was, of course, referring to Lauren. His method of gaining attention was somewhat successful in that it caused me to turn around.

"I pay you ten camels!" he shouted even louder.

"What?" I didn't know whether to be amused or angry. "She's not for sale!" I hollered, then turned back to Lauren to laugh it off. It was funny, after all, to think that a beautiful young woman could be traded for a beast of burden—ten of them!

Of course, the offer wasn't earnest. Turkey doesn't even have camels. But the expression, apparently one that is commonly thrown out with no malice intended, does say something about the status of women in Turkey, which is unique in bridging European and Middle Eastern standards of living. Interestingly, Turkish heritage would suggest a highly esteemed view of women. As far back as 1420, during the Ottoman Age when customs were dominated by Islamic law, education was considered a precept for all Muslims, women and men. When the Republic of Turkey was formed, many well-educated women played prominent roles in the country's formation. As the first secular state ever formed among Muslim nations, Turkey has granted women equal rights in voting, marriage and divorce settlements, and employment.

And yet, Turkish women today still cope with the effects of traditional patriarchal values in many aspects of their lives. Household and familial relations highlight the subordinate status of women that still underlies most aspects of the culture. In other words, what the law upholds doesn't always translate to everyday life. In fact, a commonly held belief of Islamist legislators is that a woman's role is that of mother and homemaker. Arranged marriages are still common in the country-side and among more traditional, religious families.

Well, that wasn't happening here. Lauren and I turned purposefully toward the next booth, ignoring the men and placing our attention upon the wares for sale. We bought a few trinkets and decided to return to the Gemir Palace. We were tired. A taxi was definitely in order this time.

It was only three o'clock when we arrived at the hotel, and we thought it might feel nice to indulge in that Turkish bath we had been looking forward to. The guidebooks had pointed it out as an experience not to be missed if you wished to fully immerse yourself in Turkish culture. When we asked for directions to the bath recommended in our guidebook, the concierge pointed out that this involved returning to exactly where we had come from and reminded us that he knew of a closer, local bath that would give us a more authentic experience. More authentic? Perfect. Just what we were looking for. He kindly called and let them know we were coming. Very appreciative, we thanked him. We were excited!

The directions provided were walkable, but that didn't prevent us from having yet another frustrating experience of being unable to locate our destination. We approached a local merchant who directed us to a short street which was little more than an alley. The building was small, gray, and made of cinder blocks covered in part by plaster. In the late afternoon dusk, the call to prayer could be heard, providing just enough eeriness to cause hesitation.

"Well, what do you think?" I couldn't help lowering my voice, sensing a cautious attitude was in order. We could see people approaching the front of the building. The men walked through the door, while the women were entering from a separate location that we could not yet see. No one looked American, or even European for that matter. This was a true local joint.

"I don't know, Mom. This just seems a little weird." Little did we know how weird it could be.

"Well, I say let's give it a go. We're here, after all."

We continued to the end of the alley and turned the corner toward a small women's entrance. In the reception area, it was obvious that no one spoke English. We glanced up and saw that the second level of the building was open and there were small wooden stalls positioned around the perimeter of the wall. Short curtains on metal rings provided the only privacy. It reminded me of small cells in a prison. A stairway led to the upper level, and we saw women going up and down dressed in thick white robes and flip flop slippers.

I tried explaining to one young woman who knew a little English and appeared to be in charge that we had never done this before. That was all Lauren needed to hear, and she began voicing skepticism.

"Mom, I don't think they understand what you mean," Lauren suggested, hopeful that I could be easily swayed from proceeding.

"Nonsense, they understood when I asked if they took

Mastercard!" I tried to be encouraging. "Will you help us to know what to do?" I asked, trying to appeal to a sense of customer service.

"Of course, of course," the woman assured, nodding to an assistant clothed in a blue shirtdress with white shoes. I felt a little like I was in a clinic.

This was no spa like I had visited. Still hopeful, I paid our fee, and we were led by the middle-aged Turkish woman in the blue dress upstairs to our changing room. Although there were several rooms available, she put both of us in the same room, gesturing for us to take off all our clothes and don the robes and slippers before returning downstairs. Apparently the entrance to the bath was on the first level.

"It's okay, honey, I'll just turn around while you change," I managed. By this time, Lauren was feeling trapped. She submissively and quickly changed into her robe and slippers. I changed as well.

Feminine modesty is a virtue indiscriminately possessed in Western culture. Historically, American women have evolved from a fairly Puritan sense of discretion when it comes to dressing, to one where almost anything goes. Of course, most are familiar with Middle Eastern Muslim requirements for modesty among women, from covering the hair, to extremist Islamic governmental requirements of covering the entire body.

Naturally, culture often predisposes the prevailing mentality. Technically, the Quran doesn't require burkas or even head scarfs, but does emphasize the concept of decency and modesty on the part of both sexes. Of course, all of this should be understood in its relation to men and in the context of patriarchal society. Typically, the virtue of modesty is honed to prevent men from becoming "sexually misled." This certainly wasn't going to be a problem in our present situation—there were no men on this side of the building. And yet, Lauren and I were both very uncomfortable with the idea of undressing in each other's presence. I blame it on the Puritans.

Our attendant took us back down the stairs toward the bath. We understood that there were several steps involved in the experience, but we were not exactly sure what to expect. We entered the room, warm steam enveloping our faces. The room was round, with elongated sinks lining the walls. Small benches provided seating. A sink was situated to one side of each bench, and cool water ran continuously from the faucet. In the center of the room was an extremely large marble slab able to accommodate at least a dozen people. Women were reclining in various positions against the stone, allowing the heat of the marble to penetrate their skin while the steam seeped into their pores. The thing is they were all naked. We still had on our robes.

The lady motioned for us to sit on one of the small benches, one beside the other. By this point, I was having an out of body experience. It's one thing to be naked in front of a bunch of strangers who you will never see again. It's quite another to be naked in front of your 22-year-old daughter! The attendant extended her arm to receive my robe. I obediently sat down, practically cowering in an attempt at some form of modesty before my daughter. She exchanged my robe for a small cloth and vessel. Lauren refused to give up her robe, standing paralyzed by anxiety. Finally, she lost it.

"I can't do this!" she cried, tears beginning to fill her eyes. "No! No! No!"

Well, that was affirming. One look at me, and she takes off in utter humiliation. The lady, not understanding at all what was happening, left me to myself with my cloth and cup and ran after Lauren. Timidly, I filled my cup and poured it down my chest, completely uncertain whether this was protocol. I was embarrassed and feeling vulnerable, plus I was attracting some attention from the gals on the slab. Clearly, I didn't know what I was doing. After a few more feeble attempts to water myself, I came to my senses, retrieving the towel that had been hung on a hook behind me and wrapping it around myself tightly. Lauren was seated just outside the door, crying into a box of tissues.

"I'm so sorry, honey. I had no idea…," I stammered. She only shook her head and continued to look at the floor. Right, I was still robe-less.

"Let's just go get dressed." No words were spoken. We ascended the stairs and put our clothes back on.

In the meantime, we had caused quite a stir among the clientele. Seems this never happens. I tried apologizing profusely, but the offense appeared unforgivable. The woman who spoke some English returned our money. I was glad I had purchased a necklace with the "evil eye" engraved upon it; we were certainly not sent off with well wishes.

We were emotionally exhausted. Lauren, who hadn't eaten all day, was also beyond the point of being hungry. She was tired and mortified. I couldn't help feeling like it was all my fault. We walked down the now familiar pedestrian street in silence. After about 15 minutes, I decided to venture a suggestion.

"How about we get something to eat? Maybe we can find a pizza or something? Something really un-Turkish?"

To my great relief, Lauren smiled and nodded her head yes. That one small gesture was all it took to break the wall of silence between us, and we finally began to giggle. From there, we laughed until we were nearly hysterical and causing a scene. The range of emotion we had experienced that day returned in a solid rush that broke us down to our real selves. We found an Italian cafe and shared a pizza, eating, drinking, and taking turns sharing our surprise and embarrassment over the intensely awkward situation we had just endured. We walked back like two college buddies to our hotel for an early lights out. We certainly needed it. I lay back heavily upon my pillow and breathed in deeply.

I was forgiven.

CHAPTER ELEVEN

# she knows me

—

My FIRST MOTHER'S DAY was celebrated in the anticipation of motherhood. Scott and I were living in Oklahoma City, and our first child was due the following September. Technically, I wasn't yet a mother. However, my mind was flowing with my body in the miracle evolving within me, and I was changing on that first Mother's Day.

I wonder how many mothers have similar emotions before the birth of their first child. The physical reality of another life growing within my body was overshadowed by the emotional and spiritual import that comes with sustaining that life. The "quickening" I felt in the first movements of our baby shifted any worries I had previously entertained to my now and forever most important concern—the life of my child. What an amazing and wonderful metamorphosis!

*Dear Lauren,*

*I think you really know me now as your "mommy," and you prefer me to anyone else. It's hard to explain the joy I feel when you smile—it's just so...genuine or something! You really are a beautiful baby, and I'm sure you'll be a beautiful child, too. I love you so much and love being your mommy!*

*—LETTERS TO LAUREN, JUNE, 1987*

It was Sunday morning, Mother's Day, and we woke early for the last leg of our journey in Turkey. Before leaving for the trip, this was the excursion I anticipated most. We were taking a plane to Turkey's third largest city, Izmir, on our way to visit Ephesus, which is approximately 45 minutes from the Izmir airport. There would be so much to see and learn today. What a gift!

It was a very short flight from Istanbul to Izmir, and our guide was there to greet us as we deboarded the plane. Introducing himself as Emra, he escorted us to the car and began preparing us for what we were about to see.

"Ephesus originated in ancient times as a Greek city and later became a Roman city, one of the largest in the Mediterranean," he explained. "It's most famous for the Temple of Artemis, which was completed in about 550 B.C. and considered one of the Seven Wonders of the Ancient World."

"Artemis..." I mused, struggling for a moment to recall what I knew. "Oh, yes!" The middle-aged light bulb flickered. "Isn't that the temple where Paul preached? Wasn't that where the riot of the silversmiths took place?" I was excited now. "I can't wait to see it!" I exclaimed.

"Unfortunately," Emra said apologetically, "it was destroyed in 401 A.D.; however, we will be able to see its ruins," he added optimistically. "So you know the story of the Christian Bible?" he asked.

"Yes," I responded with some level of importance. "St. Paul was telling the people of Ephesus not to believe in Artemis, but to believe in Jesus Christ, of whom there were no idyllic images to sell. Many of the people accepted Paul's teaching, thus threatening the livelihood of the artisans who created the silver idols of Artemis sold outside the temple."

"Ah, yes, so you say! It is true!" he responded enthusiastically. Building upon my obvious interest, Emra continued, telling us that Ephesus is also one of the seven churches of Asia referred to in the Book of Revelation. Legend suggests that it was the home of the apostle John and that the Gospel of John was written there.

Tourists and archeologists alike are astounded by the ruins that have been unearthed in Ephesus. The Library of Celsus, originally built in 125 A.D., has been reconstructed from all its original pieces and gives a good representation of the city's original splendor. Emra described Ephesus as the world's largest excavation site.

It was sunny and hot, and the white stone of the ruins reflected the light to make the crumbled city appear heavenly. We walked the same stone pavement as St. Paul, our guide pointing out the individual tiles scattered along the path. "Each of these half-inch tiles was placed against the others by an individual craftsman to form the three-by-three-foot stones we walk upon," he explained. "They have survived thousands of years." We continued to walk, looking down at the ancient art that humbly bore our weight. Sauntering in and out of ancient public baths, houses, courts, and libraries, we paused to consider the antiquity before us. Some of the structures were from 300 B.C.

"It's kind of mind blowing, isn't it?" I remarked. "The ancient Greeks and Romans were amazingly forward-thinking."

"I know," Lauren replied, "I wonder where we might be if the Dark Ages had never happened. It seems like we regressed so much in our evolution as a species during that time." Continuing on, we finally reached the grandest structure on the site, the theater that originally sat 24,000 people and is today considered to be the largest theater in the ancient world.

"C'mon, Mom, do your thing!" Lauren teased. She knew how much of a highlight this was for me. After all, St. Paul had preached on these very stones.

"Oh, Lauren, really…" I resisted half-heartedly.

This was my Disney World. I had spent the last 20 years of my life studying the Scriptures, four of those years involved in post-graduate work. This was my thing. I descended the crumbly steps toward the center of the platform below. Lauren remained where she was, hoping to confirm what we had been told about the acoustics. Apparently, a pin dropped in the center of the platform can be heard even by those seated at the top of the theater. Unbelievable. Reaching the bottom, I turned toward her, raising my arms for effect. I didn't quite have the nerve to attempt any sort of speech. I looked from side to side and noticed several people close by. My shyness got the best of me. Oh well. It was worth the picture, and I gave Lauren a pretty good laugh. We returned to our group to take the ancient path back to our very modern parking lot.

She knew me. There are many rewarding parts of motherhood, but one of the best is the day you realize you can let go and be yourself. Over the years, I had gradually relinquished the maternal tasks of feeding, nurturing, and disciplining my children, always maintaining a position of positive control. Their lives were now their own, and I was free of my authority over them. In reality, the past two decades had done as much for me as it had for them. I had really grown up along my journey of motherhood, including making giant strides in my spiritual life. Whether my children had initiated this growth or had simply watered the seeds, I can't be sure. Who knows where I would be without them? The point is, I was keenly aware on this particular Mother's Day that I was in the presence of not only my daughter, but also a dear friend who knew me in a way most do not.

As we arrived at the legendary home of Mary, mother of Jesus, I was struck by the singing. Emra moved his finger to his lips, motioning for us to stay quiet as we walked past an outdoor Mass in progress. I gazed upon the gathering, wishing I could join, for we had elected not to attend Mass that day in lieu of touring Ephesus. There were about a hundred people standing under a slatted pergola that dripped with tiny white flowers on vines. The scene was mesmerizing. Whether or not this was truly Mary's home, we were indeed upon holy ground.

"Look, Mom, it's Mary's dog!" Lauren teased. Indeed, a beautiful reddish-brown mutt lay peacefully on the sidewalk that led to the entrance of the abode. He lifted his head to be petted, and Lauren obliged. There she was again, that little girl.

One by one, we were allowed to walk through the lowly structure, ducking our heads to get through the entrance. I looked about quickly, not wanting to infringe too much upon the other tourists' time to walk through, and was touched by the modesty of the stone and clay home. The legend of Mary coming to this home recalled the Scripture passage at the foot of the cross, in which Jesus commissions the beloved disciple (traditionally known as John) to take care of his mother after his death. It is a well-respected opinion that John, the apostle, did return to Ephesus, and it is within the realm of possibility that he took the mother of Jesus with him and cared for her. I allowed myself to believe and absorb the wonder. Mary, the mother of Jesus, was here. More than that, I was here with my own daughter. It was the most beautiful Mother's Day I could recall.

We walked along the outer wall of the house which was covered in small pieces of tissue and cloth, evidently containing the prayers of faithful pilgrims who believed their intentions would invoke Mary to intercede on their behalf. There was also a small pond fed by a spring running alongside the home. Modern faucets allowed us to draw water from the spring, and candles were set within the shallow ponds for people to light. Their precarious positioning, fire leaning toward water, reminded me that prayer is a risk similar to placing fire before water. Prayer disposes us to believe the impossible. I walked a little way apart from Lauren, placed my coins in the tin, and took a candle. Placing it in its stand, I took the fire from the light of another's prayer, and placed it on the tip of my candle. "Dear Lord, bless my children this day. I thank you for allowing me to be a mother. I love them so much." There it was, simple. Nothing else needed to be said. Walking back, I stopped to take a drink from the spring and returned to Lauren's side.

"Happy Mother's Day," she smiled. While I can't say for sure, I imagine she was probably mildly entertained by my ritual. I really had tried not to overdo it, but something in my spiritual depths had been moved that morning. And while she couldn't completely understand, I believe she knew me well enough to have shared something of its meaning. In any case, she respected what she did understand, and I knew that she shared in my contentment.

CHAPTER TWELVE

# *weaving a life*

—

*Dear Lauren,*

*It's Christmas! What could be more fun than watching a five-year-old wake up on Christmas Day? Your eyes were as wide as saucers when you came into the room. Presents everywhere! It seemed a bit overwhelming to you, and you headed straight for your stocking that bulged with smaller and more manageable treasures. I love the stockings my Aunt Peg knitted for you and Andy. They're big and stretchier than they first appear. Daddy and I stuffed them full of lots of good things.*

*—LETTERS TO LAUREN, DECEMBER 25, 1992*

WE WERE APPROACHING THE END OF THE TRIP, and we had one final stop. Between Ephesus and Izmir was a small village that served as a quasi-tourist attraction. Perhaps a dozen small homes formed a crescent around a central meeting square that contained a couple of picnic tables, a few shade trees, and small bushes of prickly leaved flowers. Three older gentlemen who were sitting around a well looked up with interest as our car drove up to park along the weedy grass. The heat that had begun to steam us in Ephesus was now on in full force, and it hit us with purpose as we opened the car door. Emra greeted the men in Turkish as they approached, embracing them with affection, laughing, and nodding his head up and down. He pointed at the table, appearing to ask for something specific. The oldest of the three clapped his hands together knowingly and disappeared to one of the homes. The other two returned to their conversation, and Emra invited us to sit down at the table.

"This village is the home of my fiancée," Emra explained. "They love it when I bring Americans here. Such showoffs!" he chided.

"Oh, how nice that you are engaged!" I congratulated him. "Where is your fiancée living now?"

"We met through our families," Emra explained, putting his arm around one of the old men. "She now works for a carpet cooperative near Izmir and has an apartment there. That man is my future father-in-law," he said, referring to the one who was now returning carrying a bottle in one hand and a large tray in the other. "Ahmet, please welcome my guests today!" Emra gestured toward us directly.

We exchanged smiles and head bows since neither spoke the other's language. With a ceremonial gesture, Ahmet raised the tray above his head before presenting it upon our wobbly table. There were several small glasses filled with a very cold, clear liquid that formed droplets of water on the outside. There were also some small bites, which Emra explained were zucchini fritters and olive pita, a very popular appetizer in Turkey.

"What else have we got here?" I inquired, referring to the drink. Emra smiled and raised a glass.

"This," he said proudly, "is *raki*!"

"*Raki*?" Lauren raised her eyebrows and tilted her head slightly, obviously a bit skeptical about the small glass, knowing they are ordinarily reserved for powerful drinks.

"*Raki*!" Emra repeated and offered us each a glass. "This is Turkey's national drink!" he explained. "You must try it."

We were both pretty hungry, and looking at my watch I saw the reason why. It was already two o'clock, and we hadn't eaten anything since we left Istanbul. I was a little concerned about the effects of *raki* on an empty stomach. But we decided that, rather than argue and perhaps insult our Turkish host, we would both give it a try.

"Cheers!" Lauren hailed before she downed the *raki* like a shot. Her face was worth a picture.

"Hey, you look way too good at that!" I teased, smelling my drink before I tasted it. It smelled a bit like licorice, and Emra told us that in fact it was flavored by anise, a licorice-tasting spice. It's made with either grapes or figs, and we were told that it truly was the national drink, surpassing the consumption of wine in Turkey by quite a bit.

"Here goes," I said, unaccustomed to drinking this way. (I prefer wine that can be sipped leisurely!) The warmth of the thick liquid moved quickly, from my stomach to my chest to my head, and I knew right away we wouldn't have another drink. Diving into the appetizers, we finished the plate in a matter of minutes. Emra was more content with his *raki*, and allowed us the pleasure of indulging in our food. The sun seemed a little warmer, the company a little more humorous, and the food delightfully delectable. We were having a great time.

After finishing lunch, we were led to the weaving station, where some young women and several older women were busy about the work of making carpets to sell. Historically, the Turks were among the earliest known carpet makers, utilizing the double-knotted Ghiordes style that dates between the fourth and first centuries B.C. Since the 19th century, there has been tremendous demand for Turkish carpets all over the world, but making carpets still continues as a domestic tradition. In Turkey, only women weave carpets (they do allow men to repair them), and for centuries village women have woven carpets for family use. Emra explained that rugs are often made as a type of journal, depicting the hopes for the weaver's future. Obviously, they are much more than utilitarian objects!

"So, why doesn't your fiancée work here and sell her rugs?" I asked.

"Rug making is a big business in Turkey," he replied. "Over 95 percent of rug making takes place in small factories to make it more affordable for people all over the world."

"I guess that makes sense," I agreed. "It's amazing, though, that there are still some women working out of their homes."

"Yes. They work very hard. They still have to keep their house and raise their children at the same time they are weaving. Usually they are busy with weaving 12 hours a day in the summer and at least 8 hours a day in the winter."

"Why the difference?"

"The women need natural light to weave. Once the lights go on, they stop working!" he added with humor.

Generally speaking, women remain anonymous artists of the extraordinary carpets that are imported and sold all over the world. Lauren and I were impressed by the skill and humility of the women as they swiftly moved the looms side to side, their fingers dancing along the fibers of yarn. We saw how silk comes off larvae and learned that one mile of silk is created from each one! Amazed by the lack of technology implemented to achieve these results, I couldn't help expressing my astonishment.

"This takes so much patience, even just to watch," I said with a deep breath.

"Sit down, sit down, please," the woman in charge gestured. We complied, sitting next to each other on a bench the length of the carpet being woven. She invited us to give it a try, helping us twist the yarn around our unpracticed fingers and instructing us in a simple weave around the loom. The carpets that surrounded us on all sides were gorgeous. The depth of the shades seemed to defy the ordinary adjectives "red," "blue," "purple," and "gold," drawing us into their intense color, alive in originality.

"Do you sell these?" I asked, looking around the room and opening myself up to the bait.

"Oh, yes, yes," she responded. "But not so many. This is a small business. Most of the young women here are creating their dowry."

"Their *what*?" asked Lauren. I'm sure she only knew the word "dowry" from historical fiction novels.

"Many families have no money," she explained, "and the girls, they learn this craft, and they create a beautiful rug for their future betrothal and marriage."

"Really?" Lauren still couldn't comprehend having to pay someone to marry you. "They all do this?"

"No, no, not all young women," the matron smirked. "Times change, you know. These women, who make these rugs in places such as ours, many live far from the city and such things."

Just then a young woman entered quietly and sat on the bench at the side of the room. Nimbly, she began her work weaving yarns that had been previously twisted together from silk strands. She had no pattern to follow in front of her, working from memory to create this particular design.

"This is Adalet," the matron of the group provided. Immediately, the young girl stood and faced us. "She will be married next year, and she is one who is creating her rug for her new husband."

In Turkey, I learned, marriage is universal. Very few Turkish women stay single all their lives, less than two percent, and divorce rates are very low. I wondered how much this had to do with the influence of the extended family and the popular village culture.

"Congratulations!" Lauren exclaimed, and Adalet seemed to understand. She smiled widely, murmuring her thanks, and then returned to her work.

Lauren and I exchanged glances and returned to the work of our hands. Nimbleness was not our strength today, and we laughed at each other's mistakes. We did eventually manage to have some success, and the women who had gathered around us clapped and smiled. Even Adalet stopped her work to help. We felt a part of them. It was nice to be included in a small women's gathering where acceptance and hospitality were the norm. Still, it was hard to imagine living in a culture that still thrived on negotiated betrothal contracts and resisted equal partnerships in marriage. Nevertheless, our time with them went by too quickly.

After hugging our newfound friends goodbye, we walked back toward Emra who had wandered toward the picnic table. No doubt he had had enough of women and weaving. Hopefully he had played it cool with the *raki* and was still able to drive our car. Everything seemed okay, and we jumped in the car to return to Izmir and our final night in Turkey. The serendipity of our encounter with the Turkish women was not lost on me. As we walked toward the car, I turned back to catch them standing and watching us leave. I waved and they waved back enthusiastically. As women, we had shared the simple pleasure of being among one another, and it seemed a little sad that our time was cut so short. I think Lauren sensed it too.

"I wish we could have made something to take with us," she said.

"Honey, that would have taken years! At least for me," I laughed. "But I know what you mean; the pictures just won't do it justice."

"I really liked those ladies a lot," Lauren added.

"I think the reason we had so much fun with them is because they were so easy to be with. Learning something new wasn't as stressful as it can be sometimes. I think it's the "woman factor," I remarked.

"Woman factor?" she chided. "Now you're sounding a bit sexist, Mom."

"Well, how would you describe it?" I asked her.

"I don't know," she said thoughtfully. "It just felt easy. They were so calm and helpful."

"I guess I think that's why women so often gather in groups to do tasks that might be boring if you did them on your own. I remember when I was a girl, quilting groups were the big deal. Now I think there are all kinds of groups," I explained.

"Like your mothers' group? I remember when you used to go to that every week at church. You took us with you and left us with a babysitter in the church nursery!" she gently admonished.

"You're right, I did. But I needed the companionship and support of other women, and that was where I found it. My task then was to be the best mother I could be, and those women helped me along the way," I reminded her.

"I guess I get it," she conceded. "Maybe it's just that I haven't really understood the need before now. It seems so natural for women to be together." She added, "My only groups have been sports teams and maybe Girl Scouts when I was younger, and the sense of camaraderie was definitely different."

"Well, I imagine the companionship of other women will become even more important as you grow and change in adulthood. Like you said, it's natural."

We ended our conversation and quietly looked out the window at the Ephesian countryside.

—

*Dear Lauren,*

*High school graduation! Wow, it seems impossible to believe you have reached this milestone and are perched to fly off to bigger and better things. It's such an honor to be your mother on this day. It feels good to think I have been a part of the creation that is "you." I am so proud of you, and I hope and pray that the beautiful colors inside you will only brighten as you grow into womanhood.*

*–LETTERS TO LAUREN, JUNE, 2004)*

I daydreamed along the way, comparing my maternal journey to an artist crafting a beautiful rug. Beginning with only a vague understanding of what my final creation might be, I weaved my spirit in and out of my children's lives. Along the way, I hope I added texture to their God-given personalities. But ah! I have had to ponder how I will complete my task. Binding them with love, loyalty, and devotion, I admit at times I thought I was finished and could simply appreciate my marvelous creations. But I have discovered the relative smallness of my impact upon on my children. Rather than an artist, a mother is more of an instrument, like the brush or the paint or the loom. Without a mother, the picture would not be as beautiful, nor could the rug be woven, but mothers are not the only brush used, the only fiber collected, nor the only color incorporated. And the creation is far from finished. No doubt that fathers, brothers, sisters, husbands, and children will add dimension. But other women will also add brilliant colors to the palette and allow the creation to breathe life and energy. I think this is something Lauren was beginning to consider on that day.

On our drive back to Izmir, I wanted to try to capture the beauty of the rolling hills that surrounded us. This place that had cradled human beings since the beginning of their existence was as beautiful and mysterious as it was interesting. When we reached our hotel, I was thrilled to see we were on the edge of Izmir Bay. The sky was cloudless, and the water churned up white tips in the breeze. There was a walkway along the bank of the bay where children were flying kites, families were picnicking, and couples were walking hand in hand. Lauren and I decided to take a stroll before we returned for dinner. We planned to get back early in order to meet our airport driver at 3:30 a.m.

"Are you ready to go home?" Lauren asked.

"I guess so," I replied. "I really miss Dad. Wish he could have seen some of these things, too."

We came upon a waterside pub that had an outdoor patio and decided to stop in for dinner. Our meal of choice was pizza for the second time on our adventure in Turkey, but this time we decided to imbibe the local beer.

"What's good beer here?" Lauren quizzed our waiter.

"Oh, you must try Efes. It is the best Turkish beer ever made!" He sold us. And why wouldn't he? If we could handle *raki*, we could certainly take on Efes! In fact, he sold us twice. We enjoyed our drinks and our pizza and took some final photos of ourselves by the water. Ephesus had been a wonderful experience, one that neither of us would forget. It was hard to believe it had only been one day; it was truly a place of wonder, mystery, and grace.

Walking slowly back toward our hotel, Lauren was quiet.

"Well, this it," I remarked. "What's your biggest takeaway?"

"From today or the whole trip?" she asked.

"I know what you mean. The trip has been full of so many experiences! It seems like I could write a book about it," I pondered.

"I don't know, Mom. I guess I'm just so glad you came. I would never have been able to do this on my own."

And there it was. All the sights, people, and feelings during the trip had been amazing, but the most incredible part of the trip had been the experience of sharing it with one another.

I opened the door to the hotel, allowing Lauren to enter. We made a quick stop at the desk to order a wake-up call and proceeded to our room for a couple hours of rest. Turning off the lights that night, I was acutely aware of the exhaustion that is a part of traveling. More than that, though, I was thankful for the opportunity of the trip. It seemed like I had barely closed my eyes when I heard the phone ring.

"Honey … it's time. Lauren? Lauren!" I shook her shoulder gently. She had slept right through the ringing of the phone between our beds.

"Okay," she mumbled.

Dressing in the silence of the early morning, we barely exchanged glances. Our taxi arrived right on time, and we managed to finagle our way to the airport without incident. Finally it was time to board one last plane together.

We arrived in Istanbul and disembarked, each now going in a separate direction.

"Safe travels," I hugged her tightly. "Tell the girls I said hello," I reminded.

"I will, Mom. I love you," Lauren assured. "Give Dad a big hug too, and it won't be long before I'm home for good!" I think she was reassuring herself as much as she was me.

"I love you too, honey. Bye!"

"Bye," she waved and smiled, turning toward her gate.

And we were each on our way home.

CHAPTER THIRTEEN

# alone with my thoughts

—

What's worse than being alone in an airport? Being alone in a foreign airport—in Larnaca, Cyprus. What's worse than being alone in a foreign airport in Larnaca? Being alone in a foreign airport in Larnaca for 11 and a half hours. On top of that, the elevator between the two floors of the tiny airport was broken, and I had two heavy bags (one of Lauren's things to take home) and two carry-on bags to tote around until the check-in desk opened in the morning. Not to mention the food court (which was on the second floor while I was on the first) closed in an hour, and the only thing to sit on were the chairs in said food court.

This was going to be a tremendous lesson in patience. The crazy part was that I could hardly wait for a flight that left in 11 and a half hours, only to land in the Frankfurt airport and wait another five hours for my final plane home.

What was I thinking when I made these plans?

I had no choice but to trust that my luggage would not be stolen as I trudged up the two flights of stairs to the food court with one bag at a time. Luckily, that trust paid off. It was bad enough that I had to say goodbye to Lauren, who was happily on her way back to Nicosia. The emptiness in my stomach was more than hunger; I was afflicted with the melancholic malady of the weary traveler. The next full day would be filled with … well, filled with nothing really. Nothing but waiting and sitting. But I could still reflect, and I could still dream.

Admittedly, I had been a little nervous at the beginning of the trip about spending 10 days alone with Lauren. I was afraid it might be too much time together, and we might run out of things to say or ways to relate to one another. I couldn't have been more wrong. Though we were the same people we had always been, we had arrived at a new place in our relationship. We had shared something that bound us together in a new way, like fresh glue applied to the well-loved pages of a classic book. The journey to get to this place had involved traveling, in more ways than one. The experience of exploring a foreign land together had allowed us to traverse new, uncharted territory in our relationship as mother and daughter.

Leafing through the pages of my travel journal, I was surprised at how much I had managed to write. I recalled the sense of expectation that had surrounded me in my first few hours of the trip. Expectation, in my opinion, is a fundamentally positive emotion. Compared to dread or fear, it invokes feelings of excitement and pleasure. My anticipation of this trip had provided months of excitement and pleasure. My anxiety about spending so much time alone with Lauren had been squelched along the way, and the reality of the experience fully surpassed what I had dreamed it could be.

Closing the journal, I tried to get comfortable on the fast food bench I had claimed and rest my eyes. Here I was, back in Larnaca, where it all began just two weeks ago. Images from my time in Cyprus flickered in my mind: the crashing waves on the beautiful beach, the antics of the Cypriot dancers, the smiles on the girls' faces when I bought them dinner, even the old storekeeper who had chased after us to sell his wares. I knew that the memories would eventually settle and take on a life of their own. What I didn't know was how these same memories would shed such light on my growing relationship with Lauren. We had grown to know each other as women. And Turkey! What was born in our first days in Cyprus grew like a weed on our adventures there. These shared memories quickly became the jumping off point for a newfound friendship.

I was alone in the food court now. It was about midnight, and even the maintenance workers had found somewhere better to be. Although I wouldn't be home until late the next day, it was time to end the trip. I packed away my journal, tied my suitcases to my wrist, and tried once more to settle in. Sleep never really came, but the thought of resting for the night invoked the ritual of prayer. Thanking God for my wonderful husband and family, I offered a special intention of gratitude for my trip with Lauren and for the many moments of grace we had been privileged to encounter.

Journeys take a long time, much longer than a vacation. I have been on a journey with Lauren since the day she was born. The best part of the story could still be ahead of me; who knows?

# epilogue

*It took me more than seven years to write this small book. The story has continued; Lauren returned safely home about three weeks after my departure. I am delighted that Lauren and Matt were married in December 2012. They lived in Boston for two years, where Matt served as a captain in the Air Force and Lauren as a producer for public television. After two years, they moved home to Michigan. They are expecting their first child in January of 2018. We are so excited for our first grandchild!*

*I look forward to other stories I can write about my children. There is no greater joy than being a parent, and I thank you for allowing me to share my joy, my story of grace, with you.*

Made in the USA
Columbia, SC
26 November 2017